Praise for

IN HER IS STRENGTH

One of the rewards of an educator is to see young people grow, mature, and realize the dream for which they have striven and worked. To see Felisa follow that path has been my reward. She was an excellent student who I have observed during those maturing years as she went through high school, completing her studies at the University of Alabama at Birmingham and earning a doctorate degree from the University of South Alabama.

As Director of our church Bible school, I observed her develop and mature as she participated in Vacation Bible School and other Christian endeavors. I witnessed her development as a young wife and mother of four wonderful, lovely and talented children. In addition to that she is the daughter of a preacher and also the wife of a young, innovative and dynamic preacher. In all of these affiliations, she has been unwavering in her dedication to our Lord and Savior Jesus the Christ and to the furthering of the Gospel. To that end, she is often a featured speaker in local, district, and state conventions, teaching and expounding the Word of God. What a beautiful journey she has been led to travel.

Even now with her book, <u>IN HER IS STRENGTH</u>, she is reaching souls with the Word, ever elevating, inspiring and teaching. As I read her book, I was impressed with her modern-day, no non-sense approach to the issues we face as young women. It has been refreshing reading <u>IN HER IS STRENGTH</u>, which outlines steps in becoming a

Christian young woman, developing and producing God-fearing children, who are not afraid to proclaim the Word of God.

You will receive a blessing as you emerge yourself in this book, <u>IN HER IS STRENGTH</u>.

-Minnie Heath, Retired Educator -Tuscaloosa City School System

I applaud you Felisa for your vision to author this excellent motivational book filled with profound and practical truths of scripture, words of Spiritual wisdom and as my mom would often say "mother wit" (common sense) for such a time as this.

Reading this book, challenged my mind, renewed, and refreshed my spirit, transformed my thinking, and lifted me to higher heights in the Lord. This book is easy to read and comprehend. Reading each chapter was exciting and kept my attention and interest as to what the next chapter would reveal.

As a first-time young author, I commend you for your expertise in writing and composing this book, containing such rich information to so many in need of hearing words of truth filled with rich spiritual nuggets to live by. The content of this book is inspiring, humorous, strengthening, enlightening, and motivating. I was blessed by reading this book and I highly recommend this excellent book to readers, male and female seeking to strengthen their walk with God and with one another.

-Josephine Swift, First Lady of Elizabeth Baptist Church, Tuscaloosa, Alabama, Retired Special Education Teacher –State of Alabama, Director of Elizabeth Baptist Church Child Development

Center, President —Northwest District State Convention Women's Auxiliary

What an inspiring and practical guide for women and men who seek to reflect God's glory in their lives. Felisa's book is a challenging text for personal devotions as well as for assisting followers of Christ to grow in their walk with God. Open this book and find someone taking seriously the biblical call of worshipping, praising and serving God.

-Command Sergeant Major James A Bryant, Sr., U.S. Army, Retired and Youth Counselor of Mt Hebron Baptist Church (Acipco), Birmingham, Alabama

IN HER IS STRENGTH

IN HER IS STRENGTH

A transformational, motivational, and inspirational guide to living life in a way that is pleasing, holy & acceptable to God

Dr. Felisa Swift Washington

IN HER IS STRENGTH

Copyright © 2022 by Dr. Felisa Swift Washington

Get Fit in the Spirit, LLC, a division of CMW Productions

All rights reserved. No part of this book may be reproduced or transmitted by photocopy, electronic, mechanical, recording, scanning, information storage, retrieval system or used in any manner without the prior written permission from the author.

Scriptures taken from the Holy Bible, New International Version®, NIV®. Copyright © 1973, 1978, 1984, 2011 by Biblica, Inc.™ Used by permission of Zondervan. All rights reserved worldwide. www.zondervan.com The "NIV" and "New International Version" are trademarks registered in the United States Patent and Trademark Office by Biblica, Inc.®

ISBN: 979-8-9861864-0-5

ISBN: 979-8-9861864-1-2 (eBook)

Cover Design by Eden Enoabasi (Book_Publishers)

Author Photo by Chris Chaei and Cam Caliph - CMW Productions

Dedication

This book is dedicated to my father and mother, Rev. Dr. Vernon and Josephine Swift, who are the keynote speakers of my life, having instilled in me the fear and admonition of God; by securing and anchoring me to the Solid Rock, Jesus, who has sustained and kept me even in times of drifting.

This book derived from The Source, The Spring, The Living Water, whom my parents always taught me to drink from, my Lord and Savior Jesus Christ.

I pray that women throughout the nation and world who have a thirst and desire to live in a way that brings glory to God will find their thirst quenched and voids filled in the words penned in this book - the words spoken to me by God.

---

x

ACKNOWLEDGMENTS

If it had not been for God's grace and mercy granting me the wisdom, patience, and guidance through this intense, yet fulfilling process, this endeavor could not have been achieved. I am so thankful to God for this opportunity and for those who have poured into me throughout my youth and young adult life and encouraged me in my adulthood.

After several speaking engagements and people inquiring about how to obtain my speeches in writing (which will come in future books), I was encouraged by many to write a book; hence, I am grateful to all who planted the thought in me. I would like to thank my parents, Vernon and Josephine Swift, for their investment of God and time in me, developing me from birth into the woman I have become today.

To my most handsome, hardworking, humble, and helpful husband, C. Michael Washington, I am so grateful to God for placing you in my life and for your support throughout this book-writing journey. Whether it was cooking meals so that I could write, taking the kids out or to the office with you so that I could write, connecting me with other writers to guide me, etc. - I am thankful and I love you to infinity.

To my four amazing, loving, big-little ones, Chaei, Cam, Case, and Cylen, I thank you 'my babies' for being tolerant and patient with mommy when I yelled many days, "Be quiet, you are scattering my thoughts and I am trying to finish my book!" It is funny now, although it wasn't very funny then. We made it and I thank each of you for your understanding, care, concern, comedic imitation of mommy, and your quietness when needed so that your mother could complete this book project. I thank God for the amazing accomplishments you four have made at such a young age and the great things God has in store for you all as you seek Him first above all else. May the desires of your heart be granted, as they line up with the will of God and have the intended purpose of serving others and glorifying God always. Mother loves you!

To my mother in love, Christine Washington, my brother, Keith Swift (Lashanda), my brothers and sisters in love, Claude Washington, Doug Washington (Alecia), Cathleen Washington Desmond, my nieces, and nephews, aunts, uncles, and cousins, thank you for loving me and supporting me throughout the years and throughout this process. Even when you did not realize you were helping, trust me, you were.

To my godmother, Connie Robertson; to my amazing friends, turned sisters from grade school and college; those who have cheered me on and influenced me spiritually and prayerfully throughout this process, especially my Mt. Hebron Baptist Church Family (Acipco), our Prayer Leader, Sister Clementine Hunt and the entire prayer ministry, my home church, Elizabeth Baptist Church (Tuscaloosa), co-workers and colleagues, I say a hearty, *"Thank You!"*

To my professional and spiritual mentors, Dr. Barbara Spencer, Doris Chandler, Ruby Miller, Brenda Carter, Rosa Walker, my youth Sunday School teachers, as well as others who have played a role in my upbringing, a special thanks for your guidance, direction, prayers, and confidence in me. Also, to my spiritual sister, Tiffany Taylor, thank you for always speaking life and favor over whatever endeavor my family and I set out to do.

To those who have provided me with in-depth publishing support, Latresha Woods, Rachel Weaver, Danielle Steele Williams, Christopher

Luna, Jason Luna, Eden Enoabasi (Book_Publishers) and Brenda Fields, thank you for paving the way and providing a helping hand in this lengthy process.

To Rosie's Bakery by Rosie Lyles, thank you for my late-night treats that were just the right amount of sweetness I needed to get through long nights of writing. I truly thank God for you and your generous, loving spirit.

To my Editorial Review Team, Angela Shorter, James Bryant, Minnie Heath, and Josephine Swift, I truly appreciate you all for taking time out of your busy schedules to provide insight, in order to ensure I best captured my audience's attention with accuracy. Your expertise was the icing I needed to top the cake. Thank you with sincere love!

To my Marketing Graphic Team – CMW Productions by Chris Chaei, thank you all for allowing God to use your creativity to be a blessing to not only your mother's book project but also to the ministry of the church. May God continue to flourish everything you and your siblings touch and work hard at, all to the glory of God.

To all of my supporters, encouragers, friends, and those who have booked and supported me with speaking engagements, blessed me with kind words, prayed for me, provided affirmative comments via my social media pages, and reassuring calls and texts, I thank God for each of you.

I cannot end this section without giving thanks to some very special ladies who saw something in me at a young age that I didn't even see in myself. Thank you to the lovely Sister Nellie Crenshaw and Sister Earline Colvin who helped me to come out of my shy shell and pushed me, as a mother eagle pushes her young birds to fly. You ladies gave me the courage I needed to open my mouth and speak what doth saith the

Lord, over a decade ago, by scheduling my first couple of speaking engagements. I have been eager to dig deeper into my study of the word of God ever since. I am thankful to all of the Titus 2 women in my life, such as Sister Agnes McPherson, who is a mighty prayer warrior and awesome role model. I am also grateful to President Maxine Abrams of the Alabama State Missionary Baptist Women's Convention for the opportunity afforded me to lecture in the parent body assembly. I thank God for your confidence in me.

Lastly, if you are reading this statement, you either purchased my book or someone gifted it to you. I am forever grateful for your support of the ministry God has so graciously begun in me. I pray you are abundantly blessed by the words of God spoken to me to share with you as you begin this, your Strength Journey in Christ. God gets the glory for this book thing that He has done!

CONTENTS

ACKNOWLEDGMENTS —————————————————— xi

FOREWORD ——————————————————————— xvii

INTRODUCTION ——————————————————————— 1

PART 1: FLAWED BUT 4GIVEN ———————————————— 4

CHAPTER 1: Fled From the Law ———————————————— 5

CHAPTER 2: Fear God and Depart From Evil ———————————11

CHAPTER 3: Insecurity, Anxiety, and Worry ———————————15

CHAPTER 4: Give and Accept Forgiveness ———————————19

CHAPTER 5: Naked and Shameful———————————————23

PART 2: CHALLENGE 2 CHANGE ———————————————— 26

CHAPTER 6: Many Spectators, Few Participators ———————29

CHAPTER 7: May My Testimony Fuel Hope and Empower Others-33

CHAPTER 8: A New Taste, A New Dance ———————————39

CHAPTER 9: Challenge to Serve ———————————————45

CHAPTER 10: Challenge to Listen ———————————————49

CHAPTER 11: Challenge to Lose Weight ———————————53

CHAPTER 12: Do What the Lord Says Do ———————————57

CHAPTER 13: It's Not Yours, It's God's ———————————61

PART 3: 'B' SALT - DON'T THROW IT ———————————— 64

CHAPTER 14: Might You Be a Miriam ———————————69

CHAPTER 15: Understanding the Miriams ———————————71

CHAPTER 16: Rule Makers, Progress Haters ———————————75

CHAPTER 17: The Word of God Is Sharper – Keep It Handy -------- 81

CHAPTER 18: You Are the Salt of the World, Taste Like It ----------- 85

PART 4: P8TIENTLY AWAITING ------------------------------------ 92

CHAPTER 19: Waiting P8tiently for the Winning Season ------------ 95

CHAPTER 20: P8tiently Overcoming Distractions ---------------------- 99

CHAPTER 21: P8tiently Overcoming Suffering in Our Waiting --- 103

CHAPTER 22: Patiently Pressing Towards Our Ultim8 Goal ------- 109

CHAPTER 23: P8tiently Awaiting the Appointed Time ------------- 113

CHAPTER 24: In Our P8tience, There Is Hope and Strength ------ 119

THE CONCLUSION OF THE MATTER -------------------------------- 125

DAILY REMINDERS -- 127

A NOTE FROM THE AUTHOR'S DESK -------------------------------- 134

FOREWORD

Dr. Felisa Washington has penned a powerful, spiritually motivating book for women (married, single, working mothers, single mothers, etc.). As I turned the pages of this book, I found myself laughing, crying, nodding in affirmation, and reflecting on my personal life experiences.

Dr. Washington is the wife of my pastor, Dr. C. M. Washington; the mother of four talented children; and the First Lady of Mt. Hebron Baptist Church, ACIPCO in Birmingham, AL. She is a woman of God, a spiritual speaker across the state of Alabama, and a youth leader in the local church and state conventions. In addition to these titles, she's an accomplished nurse who has served as the lead nurse in a large school system.

If you are a woman trying to juggle through the many responsibilities of life, this book is for you. It will provide a spiritual basis for your day-to-day and give relevant scripture to guide and strengthen you while allowing you to laugh (and even cry) as you relate to the stories of someone just like you.

ANGELA SHORTER

Early Childhood Educator, National Board-Certified Teacher, Over 25 years in the classroom, Youth Ministry Leader, and Youth Sunday School Teacher of Mt. Hebron Baptist Church (Acipco), Birmingham, Alabama

INTRODUCTION

This book was birthed during the 2020-2022 Quarantine, as a self-inspiration, self-pick me up, self-motivational book, which in turn contagiously spilled over into a need to also encourage, inspire, and motivate others. I knew feeling the way I felt, even after spending three to four hours a day in the Word of God, others, especially those who had not spent any or much time with God, were either feeling the same way or maybe even worse. Knowing how I felt coming into the quarantine, which was like that of a whirlwind; a hurricane; a tornado; a shock, to say the least, I knew that I would need to seek God even more for me to hear a word from the Lord to cover, protect, and direct my family during such tumultuous times. There were many decisions my family and I were facing, those of which only God could guide us to the correct answer, as the line was thin, there was no gray area, and it was either black, white, left, or right. We needed a word from the Lord.

As a pastor's wife, I felt the tense and in-depth church decisions my husband had to make, as church building doors began to close, and the city began to shut down. As a Director of Nursing for a school system of over 19,000 students, for whom in the middle of a pandemic, I not only had to make decisions that would affect their livelihood but now I had to consider their parents, grandparents, and small siblings, to whom they could be potentially and unknowingly transporting this deadly virus. Not only that but there were the lives of the nurses and the employees that were at stake. There were many, and I do mean many, decisions to be made. With a team of kids of my own, four to be exact, schooling decisions needed to be made, and ultimately, I just really needed a word from the Lord. Talk about standing in the need of prayer! I was flat foot planted in a position where I felt stuck and could not move until I clearly heard a word from the Lord. I asked God to make it so plain to me that even a little toddler could understand. God did just that, taking me through His word day by day and speaking to me throughout the day, which gave me and my family exactly what we needed to make it through such trying times. I found everything I needed in the word of God, including strength in my weakness; hence, the title of this book, In Her is Strength.

Around the same time, I attended a virtual conference called Desperate for Jesus, hosted by the Evans, Hurst, Shirer family, whom I absolutely love. I sowed a seed at the end of the conference. In turn, I was gifted a journal; that was the beginning of my writing journey. I started writing and did not stop until every page was filled. I told my husband, that once I finished writing on the last page, the last line, the last word of my Desperate for Jesus journal, I would begin publishing my book. So here I am today, ready to minister to and encourage my fellow believers in Christ, my fellow Sisters in Christ, those who may not know Jesus in the pardon of their heart, and even those who know Jesus, yet feel like I felt, overwhelmed, disheartened, and even at times discouraged with all the many happenings and satanic attacks in the world. I simply wanted to use this platform to share Christ with others and, like David, to encourage myself in the Lord, while encouraging others.

In this book, I detail stories in the Bible that we may rarely hear about or may have never heard a day in our lives. You know the ones with names that are somewhat hard to pronounce - yes, those! In this book, I bring those types of stories to the surface. I strive to relate those biblical accounts to the here and the now and I pray you and all of your sisters, aunts, and nieces, whom hopefully you will consider doing a read-along, will be blessed in your diving in. What began as spending 15-30 minutes a day in the word of God, turned into spending hours in the word of God; hours of which have literally transformed my life. I pray the same happens to you. So, the journey of change begins…

Come along with me if you will…

Let me encourage you, my friend…

PART ONE

FLAWED BUT 4GIVEN

All have sinned and come short of the Glory of God. Yes, all have sinned, although, we often want to point the finger at y'all, as if we are perfect and have not done anything. As a preacher's kid (PK), expectations of flawlessness were real. PKs, you see, are often expected to be these perfect kids, yet PKs are sometimes labeled as the worst kids in the church, as the worst kids on the block, as the kids who would cause their parents, the preacher and first lady, a whole heart attack or maybe just a headache. PK or not, we are all flawed; however, we have the potential to rise above, for though we are flawed, we are 4given. Let's jump in ladies...

1

Fled From the Law

Jeremiah 2:32 inquires of us, does a young lady forget her jewelry or a bride forget her wedding fixings? Yet God says, my own people who belong to me, have forgotten about me. In other words, ladies, we absolutely will not leave home without our phones because they have become like our brains. Many can go ahead and admit you also 'ain't' leaving home without your eyelashes, drawn on eyebrows, wig, and the list goes on. Yet, how many days do we leave home without ever consulting Jesus, without ever saying, 'Good Morning Jesus,' without ever meditating on His word first? However, we are sure to not leave home without our cell phones, license, and purses, just to name a few. Do you realize when we leave home each day without first speaking with Jesus, we are technically fleeing from the law; hence, following the ways of the world and setting ourselves up for traps the world sets? We open ourselves up for a possible day of destruction, making ourselves susceptible to the satanic attacks that Satan concocts. The world thinks nothing about the law of Christ; however, though we, my sisters, are in the world, we are not of the world, for we are set apart from the world. Being set apart requires that we follow in the way of Christ, not the ways of this world. This world goes to and from without ever thinking about or caring anything about Christ, His ways, nor His laws or commands. Everyone for himself is the mentality of this world. All for Christ is the mentality of those who belong to Christ, because we realize that whatever we do, eat, or drink, must all be done to His glory.

What I have realized through the years is this, we are all Flawed, but we are all 4GIVEN. Let me break down what exactly this means. Let's take the word Flawed… The first two letters and the last two letters 'fl' and 'ed' together spell fled. Then there is law, smack dab in the middle. So, what flawed means to me is that we all have fled the law at some point or another in our lives. Whether we ran through a traffic light, threw on breaks going 70 in a 35 when we saw the po-pos, disobeyed our parents or boss, or went against our parent, pastor, supervisor, or boss' advice, all have sinned. Woe to those who act like they have had their act together all their lives. All have 'fled the law,' fled the word, fled guidance, fled direction, fled regulations, fled righteousness, and fled God at some point in our lives. In fact, truth of the matter be told, many of us are still running from God even now. Let me suggest to you that although we are flawed, although we have fled, God is a God of many chances, many open doors, many possibilities, and opportunities.

To those who are quick to ridicule (ridiculer), don't look to find the ridiculee in the tomb, where you buried them, because you have labeled one to death with words and concocted tales that lie, as all you will see there are remnants of what was. God works in us, He also works on us, and we become changed. So, if you look where you buried the ridiculee, who has been changed by the Almighty God, all you will see is what Peter saw and that is just clothes lying there, clothing remnants representing the sorrow and pain once worn, and it is in no way representative of the new changed wardrobe. In other words, don't look for me in the place you left me for dead, but look for me alive and well. Death has no victory over me; hence, search for me outside the tomb, with a different set of clothes on. I shall be found wearing clothes of deliverance, victory, and freedom. Chainless! Clothed in righteousness and ultimately forgiven. I will be found washed, white, pure, and shiny like gold. As you learn better, you do better.

We were all born into sin; however, Jesus died a death that freed us from sin, freed us from bondage, and freed us from death. Psalm 1:1-2 tells us, "Happy is he who doesn't listen to the wicked, who doesn't go where the sinners go or do what bad people do. He loves the Lord's teaching and thinks about God's teaching day and night." In addition, Proverbs 1 is a word for the wise, especially kids. Oh, how I wish Proverbs 1 had been embedded in me from a young age. Maybe I would have avoided some past mistakes. My hubby and I ensure that our kids read Psalm and Proverbs regularly as we find them to be key to wisdom and success in life. It is our prayer that we raise up sons and daughters, who are bold and of great confidence and integrity.

Have we any Acts 23:16 nephews who will step in with boldness when people try to throw us under the bus, due to the laws that they personally have created? In this passage, God tells Paul, I know they are out to kill you but keep doing what you are doing, keep telling others about me, keep spreading the truth. God then raises up Paul's nephew who overhears the plot to kill Paul. Paul's nephew informs Paul and is then sent to the Commander to inform him of the plan. Thank God that He will raise up some nephews to speak up when men living within the auspices of their own created law are trying to tear us apart. God will set some people in just the right place to overhear conversations and He will raise them up in boldness to run to the Commander in charge, the Lord God Almighty, who will send us to safety, as the Commander did Paul. Read this chapter of Acts 23 for yourself and realize in our most desolate situations, as we are fleeing, we must know that we are not running by ourselves, as God has placed people in places who will not only look out for us but who will speak up for us and go to the Chief Commander on our behalf, 'The Man,' Christ Jesus, who will keep us safe!

Though once fleeing from the law, thank God we are now free because of His law. So, I say to you, be ye careful of those who attempt to chain you to your past failures, past mistakes, and past mishaps. You, my friend, though you may have fled the law in the past, you are now fed by God's law as God has secured your future, your growth, and your maturity - for the afflictions of men are but temporary. David reminds us in Psalm that we will only go through the valley, we will not go there to stay. It is in those valley experiences where we find hope and our character is built and strengthened for the race of perseverance. Therefore, keep running, keep trekking, keep believing, for the race is not given to the swift nor to the strong but to the one who endures until the end.

As you flee from those things that are not of God, be reminded of Zechariah 7 when the Lord tells the people of Jerusalem to go, to flee, and to run from Babylon. He then tells them that whoever attempts to hurt you, will ultimately be hurting what is precious to me. Wow! That hurts! To know that what we do to others or what we do to ourselves, being that we are precious in the eyes of God, will break our Father's heart. I recall, as a kid, playing a childhood game, with the rule, or for this matter, "law," of which if you stepped on the line, you would break your mother's back. As a child, that's heart-wrenching to think that if we stepped foot on that line in the concrete, we really would break our mothers' back, so it was a done deal, we made absolute sure we did not step on that line. We would about break a leg to avoid stepping on the crack. In this thing called life, we too should be overly concerned that we do not step on or in the cracks of life that are set out to make us trip up. My sisters, be reminded to flee far from those things that are designed to break our Daddy's heart. Flee from the laws of this wicked world and run ever into the laws of Jesus, God's Holy Word.

2

Fear God and Depart From Evil

The power to overcome the things of your past means you must be willing to face your future without fears of the unknown. Fear only God and depart far from evil. As you take a flight from evil to righteousness, you may remember the departure, but do not allow the departure to distract you from looking forward to the landing. In other words, do not look back, lest we will call you Lot Wife, Jr. When Christ died on the cross, our sins died with Him; hence, do not allow anyone to try to crucify you and hang you to die a death that was already given on a hill called Calvary. We, my sisters, are forgiven, don't you ever forget it.

As we depart from evil, there is a fire ignited in the breaking of the chains, for the saw that broke the chains, should have also sparked a fire in us. As iron sharpens iron, sparks should fly, firing us up to defeat the enemy and enabling us to use our past as a testimony towards our future; a ticket of hope, an entrance gate of empowerment, and the best part is, get this, it is no cost to you, for JESUS PAID IT ALL. Psalm 36 defines the wicked in case you are unaware. As we learn to depart from evil, we learn to say "No" to the things of this world and ultimately, we learn to fear God only. We learn to flee from those things that are forbidden and run to those things that are forewritten, foretold in God's Holy Word, the things that the righteous do in fear of God. Many fear everything but God, and totally miss the point that as we fear God, we have no reason to fear anything else.

Just as pain cannot go unattended, we need to get down to the root of the problem, to find the cause, to determine what is festering underneath the skin, beneath the pain, so also fear nor evil can go unchecked. We cannot live in sin and feel our Savior's love. Therefore, there is so much depression, so much violence, and so much pain and hurt in the world, because so many feel unloved, as a result of living in sin. Sin moves us further from Christ; whereas, righteousness draws us nearer to Thee. When we fear something, we take note of the fear in our everyday lives, whether it means staying clear of it, running from it, or running to it in overcoming fear. Either way, fear of certain things causes us to walk, talk, and live a certain way. If afraid of dogs, we will run at the sight of a loose dog; if afraid of snakes, we will be very cautious walking in the woods; if afraid of spiders, we would surely wear gloves when decluttering, and in fearing God, we too, should live life differently from the world - cautiously, carefully going about life, seeking Christ daily for covering and guidance. If you do not remember anything else in this chapter, remember this, whomever or whatever we fear is what controls our thoughts and actions.

We must be willing to run away from those things that are evil and those things that try to keep us stuck in the past, because we serve a God who does not see our past, for He looks far beyond our past and sees us in our future, the definition of faith and hope. Past mistakes are just that, in the past, so we must learn from them and move beyond them, knowing and believing that we are fully and totally forgiven.

God propels us towards our future, which is why God told Lot and his wife not to look back. Lot's wife looked back at the enemy and all of his stuff, despite the command not to and she became a statue of salt. This is what some people would have you to be by always bringing up your past. They want you to be a statue so that your past remains ever visible, to remind you daily of your past disappointments and mistakes, a deterrent, an obstacle, slowing down the building project of the new and improved you. But God says you are forgiven. Even when they look back, don't you look back. Learn to block out the noise and the chatter that tries to turn your eyes away from God and deter you on the freeway to your future. Move forward, fear God only, and press on far away from evil, for I am convinced by 1 Cor 10:13 that God will make a way of escape from life's temptations.

Have you ever heard of a person in a house or building fire, running to the fire, instead of away from the fire to the escape route? Have you ever heard of a school system telling the students to run to the fire instead of out of the school and away from the fire? The answer is no because should we run into the fire, we will be consumed; however, should we run away to the escape route, we have a greater chance of survival. My sisters, God grants us a way of survival, a plan of escape and it is all in His word, so read it, take it, follow it, pursue it wholeheartedly and yield not to temptation for Psalm 32:10-11 reminds us that the wicked is trouble but those of us who trust in God can rejoice, be happy, and sing. Rejoice in the Lord my sisters, get your house in order, sweep up, dust, clean well, and allow Jesus to fill up your dwelling so that the evil spirits don't return with their seven other evil friends to take up residence.

Departing from evil requires that you empty yourself of those things that would keep you in bondage of emptiness and replenish yourself with things that are righteous and only of God. God is THE FIXER UPPER of our hearts and souls. Let Him have His way. I pray for us all to open our hearts and minds that God will take residence in us and fill us up so that we may be sealed for the day of redemption, as Ephesians 4:30 declares.

3

Insecurity, Anxiety, and Worry

Many of us are flawed in a way of being puppeteered by things we simply cannot control, such as things that worry us, bog us down, discourage us and make us insecure in our well-being. Let us not forget even the people who irritate us and cause us to feel some kind of way. Isaiah 7 reminds us not to be afraid, for even those who appear to be stronger than we, are weak. If your faith is strong in God, that's really, absolutely all you need. On the other hand, if your faith is not strong, your strength will run out. Notice I said strength, not strings. When we are attached to strings, those things that drive and pull us, instead of strength, the God thing that truly holds us up, sustains, and keeps us, we find discontentment. We find ourselves in a place where we do not want to be and hope not to stay long, a place of fear, anxiety, and worry. What has you attached by strings? What controls your actions? Give that thing that has been controlling you, causing you to feel insecure, anxious, worried, and inadequate up to God. God is your creator, your maker, and your designer. He made you and He knows all the ins and outs about you. God wants you to succeed. He wants to prosper you and not harm you. He wants you to know, my friend, that you are strengthened.

It is so important to give these things that are not of God but that are of Satan, the enemy, over to God to handle because when we do not give them over to God, they fester into bigger problems, bigger situations, bigger circumstances, called anxiety, worry, and insecurity. Be not like Saul in 1 Samuel 19, wishy-washy, petty, and jealous-hearted, just to name a few. Wishy-washy and insecure folk are good one day and you don't know what you will get the next day. They are well with you in one season and against you in the next season. You simply do not know what you will get from one season to the next when it comes to them. Oftentimes, this is acting out from a form of fear. Fear leaves shadows that follow us everywhere and shadows appear bigger than reality. Shadows can even at times look like monsters and in actuality, fears are much like monsters. Fears will scare you; they will chase you; they will follow you, and they will ultimately kill you if you do not take control of the evil imaginations they create. Fears can cause debilitating health issues, such as mental anguish, stroke, heart attack, and even cancer, which can be brought on by stress. They can all dwindle down to your kids and your kids' kids. Surely you do not want any of that. Therefore, we must encourage ourselves in the Lord, second by second, minute by minute, day by day, to overcome the pressures of this world.

What, might I ask could be causing us to feel like we do? Have you ever entertained the question of what or who are you allowing at your table? If we give Satan a crack, he will carve out a huge hole and even bring friends in with him. If we give him a foot, he will take a mile and he will go as far as you allow him. However, do you know God is at your door knocking and He desires to come in and sup with you and you with Him? When we allow God to come in and eat at our table, Satan has to flee, he has to give up his seat and you have to put him out for good so that he knows he is not welcome back. When we allow God in, we go from serving up some unforgiveness and unrighteousness to serving up some forgiveness and love to those who have hurt us - in our home, family, church, friendships, and on our jobs. You see, darkness and light cannot occupy the same space, they cannot both have a seat at the table. One has got to go. Proverbs 20:6 tells us a faithful man is difficult to find; hence, the reason we must keep our circles tight and right is that it can be difficult to find loyal, genuine, sincere, and trustworthy individuals. I must say, God blessed me with a great circle of friends many, many years ago. I have sisters that I truly count it a joy to have, as they exemplify all of the above. As my father often says, if you can find one or two good friends, you have hit the gold mine because good friends are pretty hard to find. Oh, but what a friend we have in Jesus. He is the greatest example of a true friend, who will go with you to the end.

In addition, we must be careful while at the table, that we don't dish out that which is not of God to those who have hurt us. We must not feed on unresolved issues but feed on the fruit of the spirit, which consists of love, joy, peace, longsuffering, kindness, goodness, faithfulness, gentleness, and self-control. Surround yourself with others who share the same appetite and eat the same fruit. Surround yourself with people who help encourage and uplift your spirits and soon the anxiety, the worry, and the insecurities will begin to diminish. Daniel had haters all around him but he had to tune them out. Daniel tuned the haters out by going on his knees three times a day. God heard Daniel, answered his prayer, and delivered him in the midst of the haters. God shut the lion's mouth and the haters were devoured by the very thing that was set out to destroy Daniel. Not only were the haters thrown in the lion's den but also their wives and children. There is a two-fold lesson to be learned here. First of all, when we stay on our knees, God will come to our rescue. Second, for the haters out there, when hating on the children of God, it will do a double whammy on not only you but also on your family and those attached to you. Therefore, be careful how you handle God's children because payday is coming for them who do evil.

4

Give and Accept Forgiveness

Past mistakes are just that, PASSED! When the announcement comes that someone has died, many say, he or she has passed. That means they have left here, they have died, they have gone home to be with the Lord. Our past sins, my sister, have passed, they have died, they have left here, they have gone home to be with the Lord where He has thrown them into the sea of forgetfulness, never to return any more. In order to receive forgiveness, we must first be willing to forgive. If we play in the mud, we expect to get dirty, same as if we ask for forgiveness, we expect to be forgiven, which only comes as a result of our forgiving spirit. Another side to this is that if you are the one being forgiven for an act that you have committed against another, you must be willing to stay far-far away from whatever it is that caused you to sin, or the sin itself. I am a lover of chocolate, but when I am dieting, I must not have chocolate in my house, or else, I will fall for it. Even in my mind, I may commit to saying what I won't do, but the fact of the matter is that if that chocolate is in my pantry and I know it is there and I realize that all I have to do is walk to the kitchen and get it, then guess what, out of convenience of it being in my presence,

I am going to walk to the kitchen and get it. In our fleeing from sin, we must depart from and refrain from any remnants that will likely call us back into the wilderness of sin. To truly get it out of our system, we must stay far away from it and not think about it, not surround ourselves with it and not have anything at all to do with it. Put if far from thee so that we are not tempted to fall into divers (many or any) temptations.

When learning to ride a bike, we may fall but we don't just stay there crying about it and we sure should not fault others for our imbalances and offset equilibrium that caused the fall. However, we get back up because we expect to keep moving and keep rolling. We are reminded in Jude 24 that God can keep us from falling. Yes, God is our kickstand, our balance, our equilibrium. Are you aware that when we forgive, we encourage ourselves; we loose ourselves and free ourselves from a stony heart and a thorny place; we prevent an imbalance, a disequilibrium, and brace or prevent a fall? We often sing the song, 'This Little Light of Mine, I'm Going to Let it Shine,' however when we fail to forgive, we cover up that bright light, we dim the light and put a shade over it; a shade of unforgiveness, a shade of shame, a shade that blocks communication and causes discord and disunity. We block the light from shining when we allow a shadow of an unforgiving spirit to follow us around, which smothers our fire of victory and causes a hindrance and hatred burn out. What could be isn't, what should be can't, and what needs to be is prevented and blocked, due to an unforgiving and bitter spirit that refuses to move past the past. We, as Moses, as Joseph, as many others in the Bible who were wronged, and ultimately as Jesus, must be willing to forgive those who have hurt us, whether in our family, church family, on the job, in our friend groups, or wherever the hurt may have occurred.

For those who are married, think back to your first big fight as a married couple. Can you recall what the fight was about? Maybe, maybe not. How about all the little ones in between? You can't tell me that you remember all of those, not unless you have an elephant's memory. My husband and I, as much as we love each other, have had disagreements in the almost 18 years we have been married, of which we could literally be in the middle of an argument and forget, like totally forget y'all, what exactly we were arguing about. Do you realize that this is what Jesus does for you and me? Regardless of how much He disagrees with our actions, no matter how far we stray away, when we come back to Him, and inquire of Him with a spirit of forgiveness, He forgets it all. He throws it into the sea of forgetfulness.

Let me encourage you today to loose yourself, not lose yourself, from the chains of unforgiveness, which weigh heavy, which is a lot to drag around, and can be detrimental by slowing you down in getting to your destination, resulting in detours, delays, and dread. Give your pain over to Jesus and leave it at His feet. Forgive, as we are one body in Christ, and be forgiven! How can one body part be mad with another? The Bible says if we have ought against a brother or sister, we should go to them in private. A foot which fighteth with an arm looketh foolish. Imagine that. We, being all as one body in Christ, all being different parts of the body but with one sameness, in one spirit, with one mind, shall make every effort to love the way that Christ loves and forgive the way that Christ forgives, for we are better together than apart, as an arm can swing but cannot walk, and a foot can walk but cannot talk. It takes all of us working together as one body in love.

5

Naked and Shameful

We came here naked and naked we will leave here. I know our folk will pick out the best of the best casket, the best of the best outfit, the best of the best make-up artist and beautician, and choose wisely the mortician who will have us looking our best, but the fact of the matter is, when we leave here, we can take nothing with us. As we came here is how we will leave here. We had nothing coming into the world and we will leave here with nothing. So why is it that we spend more time fixing up our outside when God is concerned with our inner being? The Bible tells us that only man is concerned with our outward appearance, but God is concerned with our hearts. While we are fixing up for this one and that one, this event and that event, might we remember that in the sight of God we all look naked. We are placing leaves all around us as Adam and Eve, but God sees straight through it all, as He sees us bare and naked. Also, while some are fixing up, trying to cover up flaws and all, others are stripping down to everything but Christ. When we can rid ourselves of self and are totally honest with God that I NEED YOU LORD, I SURRENDER ALL LORD, I AM NOTHING WITHOUT YOU

LORD, then we can totally move from a place of shame to the place God has destined for us to be, without a bunch of hustling to get there.

Many times, we are holding on to a lot of stuff or stripping to the things of this world, giving in to the things of this world, and giving God only a glimpse of us. Often, we give God bits and pieces when He already sees all and knows all, because He has x-ray vision and can see right through us. Give God all the fragmented pieces of your life, my sister. Give God all the puzzle pieces, and don't leave out anything because the Potter wants to mend, mold, and make us into what He has for us to be - the final product. God desires all of us.

Now, back to the stripping. If we are to strip to anything, we should be stripping ourselves of hatred, unforgiveness, malice, jealousy and the list goes on. When we fail to forgive, we fail to truly love the way that Christ loves us. When we allow all the latter to take over, God allows His anger to turn against us and we begin to look like sinful, shameful, ridiculously covered up people. Unforgiveness and all the latter will strip you of joy, peace, happiness, and even love, as your bitterness seeps through the cracks and unrighteous feelings brew.

Some of us drive these things like a maniac on the interstate, uncontrolled, swerving into others' lanes, dodging folk, speeding by, and creeping past. We are driving so fast down the road of unforgiveness, envy, and wickedness that we are destined to soon crash and even burn. Isaiah 47:14 tells us that the fire will quickly burn you up. Well, guess what? I don't know about you, but I have been burned enough by people and circumstances; therefore, I refuse to be burned as a result of my own doing, my own unforgiveness, my own lifted high and hard-headedness.

The ways of the world and unrighteousness have become like handcuffs, prisons, the escape room, to so many; hence, there is an influx of mental anguish going on in our world. Allow Jesus to deal with your strongholds, those things that have you chained and bound so that you can ditch it. Hand it over to God and choose not to swim in it but rather allow God to throw it over into the sea of forgetfulness. Otherwise, it is as if you are carrying a boulder around daily, when God wants you to cast your cares and burdens on Him because He cares for you.

When we are willing to let go and press forward, our prayer life will turn up and our daily devotion will delve up as one crying out in the wilderness from a very dry and dead place. When Adam and Eve sinned in the Garden of Eden, it brought shame on all of us, not just some of us. All of us have sinned, but Christ died for us all, that we all will live a life free in Him from sin and shame. God wants to forgive us all, so must we be a forgiving people, stripped from all the baggage of the world, naked and unashamed of the gospel of Jesus Christ. There is but one measure and one standard, and that is to be measured by not just any ole' ruler, but The Great Ruler. Hence, do not subject yourself to anyone else's standard and do not attempt to measure anyone else by a standard that you have set, but stand beside the Ruler himself and measure up only to Him. We were all once flawed, but in Christ, we do not have to be appalled. Naked came we into the world and naked we will leave here, for God will expose that which we attempt to hide.

PART TWO

CHALLENGE 2 CHANGE

I have competed in many challenges in my lifetime, from field days to Bible bowls to weight loss challenges and more. Needless to say, I have had my share of challenges. What I have found in most challenges, is that they drive you to an end goal. Most times, the end goal is to make it to the finish line, but not just make it there; however, make it there to win.

We often say God is preparing us for something that I cannot handle right now, which is true, but do you realize that God also has either previously prepared you for the right now or He is ready to send you out right now, with these four powerful words, I AM WITH YOU? As God told Moses, even in all his excuse-making as to why he was not good enough to deliver the Israelites out of Egypt, God said, "I Am sent you, and I Am with you. All you have to do is tell them what I say and do what I say." Moses, Abraham, and many more were given the torch right away and immediately God expected them to run with it. So, my sister, run and rock with it, because change is in you, and it is only up from here.

Even when you do not feel like you are enough, know that with God you are all that and some. Even when you feel unprepared, know that with God, you can do all things. Even when you feel like it is not quite your time, when God says, 'GO,' we must move and know that God is right there all the time, holding us by our right hand. He will never leave us nor forsake us, and He will not stop the good work that He has started in each of us until He has completed that which He has begun.

Might I suggest that we are not just living the life, we are living life with an end goal in mind, with a destination in mind, with a victorious result in mind, that one day, heaven will be our home, where we can live eternally with our Father, God. But first, we must be willing to train, prepare, and change. I wouldn't wear sleepers in a marathon, I wouldn't wear a sweater for weigh-in day of my weigh-in challenge, and I sure wouldn't wear a dress suit in a swim competition. Most challenges require that you change into the proper attire to secure a victory. You may show up for the challenge one way, but once you get there you are sure to compete in another way, in new attire, with a renewed and refreshed mindset, all in hopes of coming out on top, as the winner.

Infants are born into this world with parents knowingly expecting them to come into the world crying, very needful, and dependent on them. However, the parents also understand there is a change process that will take place as the infant grows. The infant will soon roll, crawl, walk, and run. They will begin to have developmental changes and growth that eventually, over time, yield them into becoming adults. As a child, I often remember older women saying, 'protect the baby's soft spot,' and 'don't touch his head.' Why, I would often ponder? This being the very fact that a child's soft spot is a weak spot and since the brain is still developing and the skull is still in the process of closing completely; hitting, bumping, or pressing that soft and weak spot could cause damage to the baby's undeveloped brain. Please believe that we all come here with a soft spot, a weak spot that God is steady grooming, strengthening, and growing in us so that we can become more and more like Him and walk in His ways, while also talking the way He talks and living the way He wants and desires us to live.

And so, I challenge you to change in order to grow properly in Christ and to secure the victory. We can prepare for the victory by being willing to change our attire, our mindset, our walk, and our talk, in order to hear our Father say, "Job Well Done!" This, my sister, is your time, your season, your challenge to change for the win in the word. My sisters, when God's word takes root in us, it is grounded and it sprouts out as we nourish it, flourish it, and water it. As it absorbs the sunshine and the nutrients, it produces fruit for the good of us and others to enjoy, as we share the goodness of the fruit God allows us to bear.

6

Many Spectators, Few Participators

In every challenge there is, you will find there are typically more spectators than participators. Why is this, one might ask? Oftentimes, we do more talking, more chatter, more looking at everyone else around us and what they are doing, than actually acting, actually participating, actually putting in the work. I challenge my kids daily to do something that will enrich their minds. They are required to pray daily, read the Bible daily, and write three things they have learned from the passage of scripture. They must also read two to three books a day and write a summary so that I can ensure they haven't lost their writing and punctuation skills during the pandemic/ virtual school. We also suggest that they research something new every day, of which they either do not know or that of which will help them in their gift and future desires. Why do I do this, one might ask? I do this because I refuse to allow the world, social media, scrolling, and pressures of society to change what we have worked so hard to instill in our kids. We do this to keep their little minds occupied because we realize that Satan is going to and fro seeking whom he may devour. We do this to ensure that as they mature, they mature in Christ and not in the ways of the world.

Is social media bad? Absolutely not! It is one of the best man-made platforms invented to offer services, minister to others, and to fellowship and network with others. However, it is so influential in the mind of those still developing that I choose to influence my kid's gray and white brain matter rather than allowing the world, through social media, to influence them. I choose God to change and shape my kids into the vessels He would want them to be so that they can be used by Him, rather than the world influencing them into thinking this life is all about them and what they want and what they need because in actuality, it is not.

This life is all about Jesus, bringing glory to His name, letting His light shine, worshipping Christ only, and bringing lost souls to Him. Hence, our kids must participate in the change that God is working in them, as they mature into men and women of integrity. Allow God to change you too, my sister. Do not be moved by the spec-haters, nay-sayers, and attention seekers. Be a participator and learn how to tune out the distractions and spectators, whether cheers or boos, as all at some point can and will become a distraction if you focus too much on what others, present-day Pharisees and Sadducees, are saying, instead of listening to what God is saying and keeping your eyes focused on Him.

I am reminded of a fella by the name of Stephen, who was stoned to death, for the sake of Christ. Stephen was a participator, whom we find in Acts 6, given the responsibility of speaking what doth saith the Lord. Even as a participator in the ministry of Christ, doing what the Lord said to do, would you believe the people got angry at him and concocted up all kinds of malice against him? The haters started doing what haters do -

hate! They caused all sorts of confusion by stirring the people up and filling their itchy ears with lies. Even still, Stephen did not let this stop him. Stephen was prepared for the task before him and so must we be.

We read throughout the Bible how God prepared His people for service. They were prepped, armed, and suited for whatever task God had given them. We see some with spears, some dressed in uniform, war gear, some with a belt, stashed with a sword on ready, and some with a sword in hand. I can even recall the men of God inquiring of God how they were to carry the box, the ark of the covenant. When we stay ready for the task God has charged us with, then we don't have to get ready.

My sisters, feed the haters the bread of life that they may be made whole and strengthened, as we find in Acts 9, Saul (the hater) changed to Paul (the Christian), who was strengthened and changed in his eating after he was baptized. My imagination sees him eating not just any food but feasting on the Bread of Life, which saved his very life. In verses 18 and 19, we find Paul participating in the change that had come over him, as we see action words, he got up, he was baptized, he ate, and he regained his strength. Paul then ran on to see what the ends 'gone be.' Hater turned participator!

It is possible to do a 180; hence, be the witness and the change that you want to see in those around you, and remember haters do what haters do. We can learn from David's wife, Michal, that haters are bothered by our happiness, by the dance in our footsteps, by what God is doing in and through us. However, do not let that stop you from your drive - toot your horn, which is God's horn, as He lives inside of you, and they will have to move out of the way. At any rate, keep it moving because your participation is required in order to make it to your destination.

We must ask ourselves, are we bearing good fruit, herbs, and medicine, with comforting and refreshing aromas? Or are we bearing thorns, and pricks, both of which are designed to stick and stab; hence, hurting people? Hebrews 6:7-8 speaks of producing a useful crop; therefore, receiving the blessing of God, as opposed to producing thorns and thistles, which we are told is worthless and of which, has the potential to be cursed and burned. Because we want to inherit the promises of God, we cannot become sluggish in our actions and participation in the ministry of Christ.

7

May My Testimony Fuel Hope and Empower Others

One thing about a good testimony is that it is often fueled by a valley, wilderness, or Red Sea experience. What I have learned through the years, is that it is those wilderness experiences that make us wise because it is those events that break us down to our knees, that send us running to the word of God for knowledge and understanding and that has us ever seeking a resolution for restitution. It is these very testimonies that God expects us to share with our kids, our grand kids, and our great-grand kids, that they may walk in the way of the Lord and come to know Him deep down within their hearts.

I cannot help but think of what a testimony Joash must have had to share with his kids, grands, and greats. Joash's legacy is a testament of what was almost taken away, BUT GOD! We are birthing kings and queens, ladies, we are birthing heirs of God that will put out exactly what we pour in. What are you pouring into your children because you do know charity and training begin at home? We cannot expect the schools to train our children. God has entrusted them to us, and it is up to us to include them in the group of people whom we empower. In fact, our kids are our priority. Shame on us out here trying to be successful at the cost of our children, many being raised by the streets, and being infused by social media. This is the day and age we live in, and it is time out and time up. It is time for us to step up to the plate, take care of our responsibilities, and empower our kids even before we empower others.

Now, back to Joash, who became the king of Judah at the tender age of seven. Don't you tell me what God can't do because what He has done for others, He will do the same thing for you. Imagine a seven-year-old as king. This was not just any king though. Joash was not just any seven-year-old. Joash had a bounty on his head as a baby. He was sought after to be killed by the very evil ruler, Athaliah, in 2 Chronicles 22, but thank God, when the enemy comes against us like a flood, He will put up a standard against the evil one and raise a Jehosheba to the rescue. Jehosheba stole baby Joash from among the royal princes who were all on Athaliah's radar to kill. Jehosheba hid little Joash in the temple of God for six years. Talk about Jesus being a fence. Joash ended up becoming a great king of Judah, while under the leadership of Jehoiada. He did what was right in the sight of God, as long as he had Jehoiada leading and directing him in the ways of the Lord. Unfortunately, soon after Jehoiada died, Joash began listening to people who led him wrong and away from the ways of the Lord.

Ladies, if we are to empower others, let us begin within our own family and ensure that it spreads abroad. What we pour into our kids is crucial to their upbringing and could potentially prevent a downfall. If we are pouring so much into them, it makes it near impossible for negative influences to have any space to add their tidbit.

I am one who can multitask, and I must say for myself, I multitask well. However, I can only listen to one conversation at a time. I can multitask, but I cannot multi-hear. If multiple conversations are going on around me, I must give my full attention to the one conversation that is vital to my understanding; otherwise, I will hear bits and pieces of all; however, I will be utterly confused. This is exactly what occurs when we are not speaking to and over our kids but when we allow them to be poured into by all the outside influences around them. Let your testimony not only be a blessing to others, let it not only empower others outside your home, but let it begin within your home and with the little people that God has blessed you with and those of whom He will hold you accountable for, ensuring you have instilled in them the fear and admonition of God.

Deuteronomy 6 makes it plain when it tells us to impress God's commandments, His ways, and His laws on our children. That means to make a mark on them. We are told to talk to our children about God's word when we sit down, when we lie down, when we awake, and to even put it on their hands, foreheads, and to write it on our door posts and gates.

Judges 13 is a really good example of what a parent, who uses their life to empower others, looks like, as we learn of Samson, a baby boy who was dedicated to God before he ever came out of his mother's womb. Samson's parents, upon learning that they would give birth to a baby boy who would have the awesome and mighty task of delivering the Israelites from the Philistines, prayed to the Lord, asking how they should bring the boy up. Wow!! Read that again. What a world this would be if only parents would ask the Lord, what should we do to bring this child up. If only we, as parents, would consistently go in prayer, seek God, and dive into the word of God to see what God has for us to do for our children. If we would consult God on how we should raise them and how we can ensure that everything they touch will flourish to the glory of God, what a magnificent and God-stained world this would be. It would be a beautiful sight to see.

Can you imagine parents, children, churches, communities, corporate workforces, businesses, and governments all working together to bring Glory to God? I am still under the persuasion, sisters, that there still lies hope ahead. As frustrated as I get when watching the news and reading news articles, I have not yet given up on humanity because God hasn't and never will give up on me. I trust God to continue to work through me and those attached to me to encourage and empower others to **Matthew 6:33,** and that is to seek God first, do right, and watch God do the rest.

As God prepares us for greatness, molds us, shapes, and bastes us, we must be willing to share our tests turned testimonies with others. Many of us have experienced right out dead situations, those times in life where it was dark, gloomy, and we felt all but in a casket. However, as God lifts us up out of the miry clay, we must share the good news that just as Genesis 50 tells us that the Physician embalmed Jacob's dead body, our Great Physician, Jesus, has done the same for us. Jesus has embalmed us in our lowest and most dead feeling moments. In other words, Jesus has preserved us, He has sanitized us, and cleaned us up. He has slowed our body down from decomposing and He has enhanced our appearance from the inside out. Don't be 'scerd' tell the good news of how God raised you up out of a dead situation. We must not keep it to ourselves.

I know sometimes we may feel like a crumb. The commercial says sometimes you feel like a nut. Sometimes I right out feel like a piece of crumb from the nut, one of which has been looked over (you know that job, of which you had to do twice as much to get). In feeling 'crumbish,' we may feel wiped up, wiped out, discarded, on the floor, swept up, trashed, and even as a crumb on someone's lips, as we are talked about and criticized, even licked up, and ate up. Sometimes, we just may even feel like a crumb on someone's shirt, shook off and shook up. Did you know that God can and God will take what appears to you to be crumbs and bake a sweet and savory cake with it?

God allows us to go through things in life to show us from whence comes our help and in order for us to serve as a testimony and to be a blessing to others. As God blesses us with much or blesses us with what are sometimes called small beginnings, God intends for us to utilize every blessing He gives us not just for ourselves, but to bless others and to be a blessing in His kingdom, showing forth His light and His glory. As God changes us, through our testimonies, we learn to follow and obey God's word and share those changes with others; hence, immunize them from the diseases of this world by inoculating them with that of which God has inoculated us.

Many just need to know there is hope though Christ Jesus. Many just simply need to be empowered. What better way to empower others than by sharing the tests that changed you, in hopes of bringing about a change in someone else. Make a difference in the lives of others, that is what Jesus did, and He expects the same of us. Encourage, empower, and hope through every test, that's the message to resonate.

Ever been stuck on an airport concourse? That is the most disheartening feeling because you have rushed, you have been stripped down from head to toe, then you finally make it to your plane only to end up stuck on the runway for who knows how long, stuck in a small enclosed space with a lot of folks you don't know and really not knowing when you will receive the all-clear to proceed to your destination. You must wait it out until the air traffic controller clears your flight. Why stand still, my sisters, when our Air Controller, Jesus, has cleared our flight?

Faith says propel, faith fasts forward, faith does not look back, faith looks up from whence cometh our help knowing that ALL OF OUR HELP COMES FROM GOD. You can soar high, my sister; therefore, stop sitting on the runway of life and take your flight because the Air Controller, Jesus, has secured the flight and He has equipped you with everything you need to soar. He knows you have been through a lot to get to the runway, so soar baby, SOAR, and do not forget about the people you see below as you fly high. Be the testimony they need to know that they too can fly.

8

A New Taste, A New Dance

For many of us, we are craving stuff that is unhealthy for us. Things we should not be consuming and some of us are right out dirty dancing with the dirty world. Some of us are surrounded by a circle of friends and even frenemies, who 'meaneth' us no good - always gossiping, always telling lies, always finding fault, and never anything good to say about anyone. Proverbs 20:19 tells us to stay away from those types of people who talk too much for they are not to be trusted. We, my sisters, are unique, we are sourced out by God, and we should stand out in the midst of others, because when others see us, they should see the BIG CHRIST who lives in us.

Do you know people will determine how you are simply by the company you keep? Mice love cheese and if you want to catch a mouse, put a little piece of cheese on a trap and see what you will get, a mouse. Maybe you aren't a fan of traps because you have little kids, well, try a sticky. Put a tiny piece of cheese in the middle of the sticky and watch the mouse and some of everything else get stuck to it. This, my friends, is exactly the way we allow the world and those very talkative people around us to do us. The world sticks a little piece of this and a little piece of that in our faces and in front of our eyes, and instead of focusing on God and all of His promises and claiming what God has put before us, we get trapped, stuck to, and glued to the things, habits, rituals, mess, and busyness of this world. My sister, God wants to give you a new taste in your mouth. God wants to bless you with a new dance that will change your attitude. If we would only ask for it, God would give it.

Before our kids ever breathed the air of this ole' world, I prayed Psalm 150 would resonate in our home. I prayed that we would birth children who would be bold and praise God on the instruments. God has granted that request and I am forever grateful, for it is all to His glory. My oldest son plays the organ, my middle son plays the drums, my baby son plays the saxophone, and my baby girl sings. God is so good; He granted my hubby and me a mini-orchestra so we can praise God with the Psalm 150 instruments whenever we get ready. All it takes is for me to start humming or singing a song and my oldest son will go to the keyboard in his room and begin playing, then the others will follow suit in their various God-given gifts. When we pray for what we want, with a sincere heart, coming from a genuine place, God will grant us our desires. I am a firm believer because I know what He has done for my family and me.

Proverbs 20:11 tells us that even a child is known by their actions. Hence, my prayer is that our kids' behavior will be reflective of God always. I know that kids will be kids, as we were, but I pray that God always keeps His hands on them, even in the midst of the 'kids will be kids' moments, producing a new taste and a new dance in their lives, one that is fresh and tasteful. Speaking of tasteful, when my youngest son was little, we had the most difficult time getting him to eat anything green or yellow.

He would make the most awful faces. It would be hilarious. As he grew older and we began to eat more superfoods, the challenge to get him to eat more veggies became easier. Now, I wouldn't say he totally loves them at this time, but he does tolerate them better and now he can eat them without the monster and lemon faces. Do you know this is how it is when God puts a new taste in our mouths? At first, it may take a little getting used to or it may taste a little bitter; however, over time, it gets easier and easier to consume, easier and easier to digest forgiveness, love, kindness, perseverance, temperance, and so on. It gets to the point that we just do it - we just eat it, dish it out, and serve it up without thinking about it.

Now, when I was in high school and college, I was shy about dancing. I felt I couldn't dance and refused to embarrass myself by getting on the dance floor. But now, But God! Over the years, God gave me a new dance; and now, I am in no way embarrassed. I don't care what I look like doing it, I don't need rhythm for it, and it never goes out of style like the Tootsie Roll and Cabbage Patch for those over 40. I have a new song, a new dance, a new step for the Lord, and so can you. Allow God to do the change in you and watch Him do the work.

If God can turn water into wine, if God can change death to life, if God can change Saul to Paul, if God can change the sacrifice of a boy named Isaac to a ram in a bush, if God can catch a bush on fire and it never burns up, then surely, you can believe, God has the power to change you. You can't change you, that spouse or parent can't change you, but GOD CAN and God will, when we submit and surrender ourselves totally to Him.

I have often found myself singing the rhyme in my mind, Liar, Liar, Pants on Fire, when I hear the same sob story, the same pitiful woe is me;

'I have to get myself together first' story from folk speaking with their lips; 'I am coming back to church' while knowing in their heart that you will not see them. We must want change for ourselves. God works with a willing vessel. He is not going to force you into anything. God is not a micromanager. He gives us His commands, but He allows us to choose as to what we will or will not accept or do.

Let me warn you that it is a dangerous thing to make a promise to God and not follow through on it. Don't believe me? Check out the Old Testament and learn of the things that will occur as a result of false promises. God's word is true. The promises and vows we make to God are to be followed through; otherwise, there are consequences that we must face.

My sisters, do not fall for the world's setup, trap, or get caught up and lost in the maze of this world. Allow God to have His way in you and watch how you develop a new song, a new taste, a new dance, and a new move. And when you get your groove back, girl, do that dance, do that dance, do it. Don't give God your scraps when you can give Him your all. God wants all of us and He wants our best.

I recall the few parties that I have attended in my life. When people went to the dance floor, they would give that dance floor their all. They didn't leave anything to ponder, they put it out there and got all the way into that dance. Ladies, if you aren't giving God what is valuable to you but expecting all of His goods, you have it all wrong. We cannot offer scraps, when He gives us a surplus. God looks at our hearts and He looks at what's in our hands. It is not about the amount, but it is about our intentions, motives, and if we truly gave it from the heart and gave it at our best. The widow gave her last, Hannah gave her only child and son

Samuel, after being barren, while praying for a child for many years, and God gave His one and only Son, Jesus. So, my question to you is, as God gives you a new taste and a new dance, what of value are you willing to give?

Psalm 149:6 tells us to shout for praise with our two-edged swords in our hands. What's in your hand? Did you know that the two-edged sword refers to your Bible, which comes to heal, deliver, comfort, and set free? So, while you are holding that remote control in hand, flipping channels to this series and that, while you are holding that cell phone in hand scrolling, might I suggest you put it down and pick up the Bible, for it has the master plan for your life. The Bible serves as our life guide, not the series and the stories we see. For when we read the Bible in its entirety, it will put a different kind of running in our feet and dancing in our legs. It will change the taste in our mouths, and it will propel us to get up and go even when we do not feel like going. A new taste and a new dance come when we commit to utilizing, at its fullest, that which God has already and so graciously given to us.

9

Challenge to Serve

In Matthew 10, we find Jesus' followers being called together as one. Oh, what a sight to see when brothers and sisters in Christ can gather and serve in unity, as one body in Christ. Oh, what a horror to see when one body turns on itself. You have seen the movies and you know what it looks like, and it is not a pretty sight. Those who are familiar with autoimmune disorders, in which the body goes into crisis mode and begins to fight itself, know that it is a painful experience. I imagine, when God looks down and sees those who are supposed to be brothers and sisters fighting against themselves, its own body, its own blood, its own brother and sister, whether an arm or leg of the body, it is heartbreaking and heart wrenching, as God desires we work together as one body in Christ Jesus.

My mentor, Sister Ruby Miller, would always say, one bad apple spoils the bunch. It is so true that many times it only takes one ill-minded person, one Peter, one Judas, one snake, one Satan to spoil, contaminate, irritate, and infect others. Matthew 10 warns us that we will be like sheep among wolves. This is why, I am not shocked or surprised when I learn of plots and schemes going on around us, but I must say it is concerning when the plots and schemes are going on right in the house of the Lord, among our siblings in the body of Christ. But that's okay, God told me early on in my serving, as Jesus told His disciples in this passage of scripture, "I have put my spirit in you, so do not be afraid of people, be thou only afraid of God."

Matthew 25:33 tells us that God will put His sheep on His right and the goats on His left. Now, I understand to be a GOAT, in today's society, is to be the 'Greatest of All Time.' To be a goat in the Bible; however, is to be cast to the left, but I want to be labeled as a sheep to the right, to the right, to the right, with no sliding to the left. When we serve as sheep, we follow what our Master commands and we are led by Him alone.

So, questions to ponder:

Who, or might I say what, are you serving?

Have you backslidden or left slidden over to where the goats are or have you been discouraged from serving, due to the wolves and the goats?

Are you a faithful and devoted, sincerely passionate follower of Christ?

Are you a trustworthy vessel?

Are you one to make excuses instead of being enthused by the calling God has placed on your life?

Are you steady looking for ways to serve or are you more so attempting to be served?

Are you one to be led by others, rather than being led in a life of obedience to serve God in serving mankind?

Are you counted faithful by God?

Can God count on you to go when He says go and move when He says move?

If God says get out the boat and walk, would you? The boat is not on dry land, ya' know? It's actually on water and not just any water, but it's on a raging, stormy, windy, out of control and current-filled body of water.

Would you be willing to get out of the boat and walk?

Would you be willing to walk to where Jesus is, or would you sell out to remain in what you feel is the safety of the boat? In other words, are you willing to get out of your comfort zone, even when it looks life-threatening and fierce?

Do you have what it takes to stand still and know that God is God, regardless of what it looks like?

Are you underestimating your true ability to serve?

Does serving appear to you as nasty, dirty, and germy; therefore, you choose to take the safe and clean route?

As you self-examine yourself, as we prepare to stand before God, instead of asking ourselves what do I want out of life, start asking God, how can I best be used by you Lord to be the vessel that you want me to be and to serve the way that Jesus served as He walked the dusty streets? Lord, what would you have for me to do? Let us seek daily to serve like Christ, love like Christ, share like Christ, listen like Christ, help like Christ, walk like Christ, talk like Christ, live like Christ, oh, and did I already say serve like Christ? When we learn to serve God with passion and eagerness, God will grant us joy and peace as we serve from the sincere desire of our hearts.

James 2:16-17 reminds us that seeing a need and not meeting the need defeats the purpose. It is as one who talks about faith but does not act on it. It is as dead as a doorknob, just as if you see someone who is hungry but do not feed them, you are contributing to their lack of nutrition and potential starvation. Walk worthy of your calling my sister. God has called all of us to good work, of which He will not stop until it is complete.

In your challenge to change, may you seek God daily for ways to serve God, the people of God, your family, friends, and community. Use your gift in doing what your Daddy, 'Father God,' gave you, and serve. No one should have to beg you to serve. In your serving, be the consolation and comfort, the encouragement and inspiration that we want to see in others when we step foot on the church lawn. Many expect it but many are not always willing to give it. Be it, serve it, and eat it, for they say, we are what we eat, and we will become that which we dish out. The platter is waiting my friend, so set the table, plate the fixings, arrange the trimmings, and serve it up.

10

Challenge to Listen

Have you ever called your kids and they didn't come? In fact, one of my pet peeves is having to tell my kids to do something more than once. It makes my blood boil because it is as if they purposely sit there waiting on my request to be stated for at least the third time before they ever move. It is as if they answer yes ma'am on the first request, they lean up on the second, they get to the edge of the seat on the third call, they stand on the fourth, but they do not move to carry out what I have requested until that fifth call, the one with a little growl in it. You know how we do it mamas, grandmas, and aunties. And don't let me get to the line, "If I call your name one more time, I'm coming in there!" That line alone really means business. Do you realize though that as much as it irritates us, it upsets Christ even more? The same expectations we have for our kids, God has for us. The same great things we want for our kids, God wants for us. In the same way we nurture our kids, God wants to nurture us in our spiritual life with His word and by prayer. God wants us to not only listen but to trust Him in our trials, in our circumstances, and by way of cause and effect. God says, do not listen to the enemy, listen to Me and what I have to say about what you are going through.

In Genesis 31, I am reminded of how Jacob was mistreated by Laban for 20 years. He worked very hard for Laban, yet Laban continued to find ways to cheat him. One day, God spoke to Jacob in a dream and said, "Go! Go back to the land of your ancestors and know that I will be with you." In Jacob's ability and willingness to listen, there was another component, which was the fact that he did not just listen and do nothing, but he listened and he did what the Lord said to do. He gathered his wives, Rachel and Leah, and their children and animals, he told them what God spoke to him, and the wives said, "If God said it, let's do it." So, they left in obedience to God. Ladies, in our listening, let us be willing to do what we are hearing God speak to and through us.

Have you ever heard God speaking to you, but questioned if it was truly God or the late-night meal you ate? I am sure many of us have felt like Samuel when God was speaking, we thought too that it was Eli calling our name. God speaks to those who listen. Do you know God's voice? We are told in the word of God that His sheep hear His voice and they follow. Many of us talk more than we listen but I would like to challenge you to change that scenario, because we must listen more than we talk.

In addition, many who listen, fail to take notes. It is imperative that as God speaks to you, you are attentive, and you are writing it all down so that when He is done talking, you can begin acting and checking off as you go. TAKE NOTES TO TAKE ACTION! We must listen to the call of God and follow His instructions, found clearly in His word. Fact of the matter is, oftentimes we listen to everyone else and fail to listen to God and follow in His ways. If you think your success comes from listening to the Jones family and trying to follow their lead and the lead of those you follow on social media, then might I let you in on a secret, my friend, success only comes from Jesus Christ and following in the footsteps He has ordered for you to take. Only through our seeking, commitment, and submission to God, will we find success, of which we will live a life of joy, peace, and happiness, found only in Christ.

Our greatest fulfillment is found in Jesus, in His presence, and in His safety, where we dwell. Now, don't get me wrong, God places many like Moses, Elijah, and Naomi on our path to help keep us grounded, those of whom speak life into our lives, those of whom share wisdom in all their ways, and I thank God for all the connections and Titus 2 women who have invested in my life, of whom I pray blessings upon blessings over. I truly believe the spirit of discernment will allow you to sense and gravitate to those people whom God has placed on the bench of the Central Park walk of your life, to help steer you on the right path and to share with you, 'Been there, done that.' It is our job to listen.

11

Challenge to Lose Weight

We have four kids, so many can only imagine what it is like when packing for a trip. In our travels, whether running through an airport or riding a long distance in the car, the baggage is packed down, there is much of it, and it becomes a major distraction when running from gate to gate or when driving trying to look out the back window. When our kids were younger, we thought, oh it will get easier as they get older, as we figured, we would not have to pack the stroller anymore, the car seats, extra clothing for mess-ups, diapers, baby formula, etc. Well, we learned quick and hard, as the kids grew, the clothing grew, the shoes got bigger and took up more room, and the children and all their baggage that they just felt they needed to take, grew as well.

So here we are running through airports, dropping stuff, can't hardly walk, nonetheless run, because we each have bags around our necks, one on each arm, plus pulling a piece of rolling luggage with each hand. Imagine that pretty ugly picture if you will. And let's just not even get into the 12-hour car ride anywhere! You know the one where the kids' knees are up to their little eyes because we have so much stuff piled under their feet and once you are settled in your seat, the real-life game of freeze begins because you are stuck in place and cannot move until the next stop, as there is not an inch of space available for you to move - so sit down, be still, and enjoy the ride, will ya'? Yeah, it's a mess.

Do you realize, this is the way our life is when we are carrying baggage around that God has not told us to bring along for the journey? Yeah, it really is a mess. God is saying you are older now. I understood when you were babies that you were simply immature. I fed you milk because you weren't ready for solid food; but now, oh my, you have grown sillier; more grown, but more foolish; more grown, but heavier; more grown, but weightier.

God is saying, get rid of all that baggage, all that stuff, before it causes you to miss your flight to the destination, where I am taking you. Rid that stuff before you miss your turn. I am telling you to go left but all that baggage is up in your window and so you can't see where I am leading you; hence, you mess up and decide to go right. God says, "Let it go." Declutter, unpack it, leave what is not necessary to carry, better yet even remove your sandals, take only your walking stick, just buy it when you get to where I am taking you to or better yet, the birds don't store up anything and they are fed daily. Do not pack it and don't store it up because where I am taking you to, I have already prepared for you, and it already has everything you need. The condo will be fully stocked with food, furniture, and fruitfulness in every area you can ever imagine or think because I am doing a great thing in you and I will not stop until it's complete, but you must exercise faith and leave some stuff behind. Faith that frets is not faith at all, its frailty. Lose the weight, leave the baggage, and just do it. Step out on Faith and keep it moving by Faith.

In your losing weight, let's briefly talk friends. If your circle of friends will not throw you a lifeline in your Red Sea or Jordan River experiences of life, if they aren't offering you a ladder in your pit or valley, you may want to ditch that circle and opt for a triangle - a faithful few, a trio. Small stands tall in action.

12

Do What the Lord Says Do

Ladies, I cannot stress enough how important it is that we are ever willing, open, available, and eager to do what the Lord says do. Some of us do partially what the Lord has told us to do, but leave another half undone. God expects us to follow all of His commands to a "T" without wavering. Don't believe it? Visit Numbers 20 with me as God tells Moses to speak to the rock and water would come out of the rock, providing water for the complaining people; however, Moses decided he would handle the rock differently than God commanded, as he hit the rock twice. God still provided the water as promised. However, as a result of Moses' disobedience, because 99 1/2 won't do, God told Moses, "You will not bring the people into the land that I have given them." On the other hand, have we any Zibas? In the book of 2nd Samuel, Chapter 9 we are introduced to Ziba. Ziba says, "I am your servant. I will do everything my master, you, the King, commands of me." Wow! What a world this would be if we were all that type of willing towards the commands and words of God.

When we came into the pandemic and realized we would be home for a while due to the lockdown (not realizing it would be this long), we bought some games that we could play as a family. One of the games we bought and had a lot of fun with is called Twister. I am sure many of you are familiar with this game. You spin the wheel, and whatever color it lands on, every family member has to plant their hand and foot on that particular color. By mid to end of the game, it ends up being a twisted-up kind of mess. In real life, many of our minds work like this game. In fact, many live their lives as if it is a game.

When we live life in a way that is exclusive of Christ, spinning the wheels of our minds to decide what we will do from one day to the next or allowing others of the world to spin our wheels for us, directing our hands and feet to which way to go, we ultimately lose focus of Christ; and we, as in the game Twister, end up a twisted mess. After a good game of Twister, I have found myself sweating, worn out, and tired, like lying down and taking a nap kind of tired. The same goes for us in this life, after playing all of the world's games, it makes for a perfect setup to slip up and be asleep when Christ returns.

Will the Master find you sleeping when He returns because you have had too much fun playing the life of Twister? When we focus more on likes, follows, shares, selfies, pictures, all these little gods, and idols than we do on God, we worship ourselves and our stuff and we lack true worship to God in spirit and truth. You do know God sees, and He knows the difference. We can fool folk, but we can't fool God.

As we seek to change, we must continue to do what the Lord says do. If you have ever broken down on the side of the road, most times, you don't just sit there. You try to figure out what just happened and you troubleshoot. In other words, you try to figure out what went wrong. Same, as we wait for Jesus to return, we don't just sit here and do nothing; nor do we do what we want to do, rather we work while it is day, because nighttime cometh when no man can work. Do what the Lord says do. Just as we would call the mechanic for our car that is broken down, call God for those times in your life when you feel broken and whatever you do, when God responds, be sure to do exactly what the Lord says do. As Nike says, 'Just do it!'

13

It's Not Yours, It's God's

We are an I, I, I, and me, me, me society - My this, my that, my day, my time. Do you realize time is not yours? Time, all 24 hours, seven days a week belongs to God. It's His time, but oftentimes we use it for ourselves and everyone and everything else, but Him. Let me ask you this, do you glamorize more than you gratify God? Do you spend more time on your outside beauty than the inside? How much time do you spend putting on makeup, eyelashes, drawing your eyebrows, etc.? Now, how much time would you say you spend pouring into your inside, nourishing your mind, your spiritual body, and your soul? This is food for thought and something that we all should consider and work on. What we are investing our time in most, is ultimately where our heart is.

I want God to know and witness the fact that I choose to invest several hours a day in His word. Typically, it only takes me five minutes or less to throw on a lil' make-up, because in my heart, I care more about my inside being right with Christ than my outside being right for y'all. If your time is not being used for the glory of God then might I suggest, reevaluating your time, your schedule, your day.

As we change, we must make time for God, because it is His anyway. As we change, we must be willing to live life the way Jesus lived. Jesus lived looking for and seeking out ways to serve others. Turn with me to 2 Samuel 19:28. We find Mephibosheth in a place of gratefulness to King David for giving him a place to stay and caring for him, even considering his grandfather King Saul and family were enemies to David. Mephibosheth says, "What right do I have to ask for what's yours?" God had given David the victory; but David used his victory to be a blessing to others, not to keep it all to himself. Mephibosheth goes on to say, I am just grateful you have made it back home safely and in peace. So, let me inquire of you, have you any room for others, or are you so swollen in self pride, in self-indulgence that you are too much for everyone else, too much for even God, too much and too big to serve? Let me tell you, God is bigger!

In our serving, we must strive to bring others to Christ. Peter preached on the day of Pentecost, and in just a little time, thousands were saved. Do you realize what you choose to do with your time and your salvation not only affects you, but it may affect others attached to you and can ultimately save or take their life? What or who do others see you chasing after? Are you chasing after God, because you do know that He will slow down and give you time to catch up, ya' know? He gives us chance after chance, but one day, just one day, after you have chased all this stuff, and chased all these people who have done nothing for you, it may be too late.

Yes, God is patient. Yes, God gives us many chances to get it right; but time is of the essence and tomorrow may be too late, so let's take care of God's business and develop ourselves by growing in Christ, instead of growing in hair, nails, and material things. Some of us are around here like Chi-chi-chi-chia, growing overnight in pride, jealousy, envy, and the list goes on, but my sisters, let us grow in Christ, go into our prayer closet, and grow into our Bible. It doesn't require we go to a beauty shop, nail shop, or mall. It's the type of growth that will sustain us on all of life's twists, turns, and roller coasters. God's business is serious and so we must treat it as such.

In the time God has allotted me, I do daily meditations and devotionals, which are so uplifting. In turn, I share what I gather from them to encourage and bless someone else. My Bible looks like a coloring book, as I have highlighted it galore, from front to back. When I highlight, I don't highlight cute. I highlight all outside of the sentence line. And so, I challenge you as you change, to change the world with 'The Highlighter' (Jesus), who shines through you! Get outside the line, outside the box, outside the four walls, and be a beacon of change that others may see and want what you have - want to serve the same God you serve. Use your time wisely and all for 'The One' who gave it to you. It's not yours - it's His. Use it for Him and all to His glory!

We read all throughout the Bible how God prepared His people for service. As mentioned previously, they were prepped, armed, and suited for whatever task God had given them. When we stay ready for the task God has charged us with, then we don't have to get ready. The battle is not ours; it is the Lord's.

PART THREE

ʙ' SALT - DON'T THROW IT

Jesus declares that we are the salt of the earth and once we lose our saltiness, we cannot regain it. We were never instructed to measure up to man, for how can we measure one who is flawed against another who is flawed? We would certainly come up negative. The world has gotten it twisted. We were simply told to Go, to Love, to Be, and to Obey and Follow. Oftentimes, instead of being the salt of the world, we throw salt, as the world. Instead of spreading love, peace, joy, many often spread lies, mess, gossip, and envy.

What I have found in this world is that some will beat a dead horse. When someone is already down, with one foot in the grave, many will put their foot on the person and help push them on into the grave. Luke 24 tells us about a woman who brought spices. She brought a refreshing aroma; but what, might I ask, do people smell when they see you coming? Is it a smell of manure (mess) or a refreshing smell of lilies? Some might say a taste of flavor, but many of us bring salt, shade, suffering and sorrow. Ever seen a person, who always brings negative vibes; hence, from the moment you see them, your heart begins to race because you just really do not want to be in their presence? Yeah, that one, because I know you just pictured the very one, who makes you do that very thing. The one you find yourself praying about in that very moment, 'Jesus keep me so near the cross that nothing this person does or says stirs me up.' You do know Satan himself will stir you up, but only if you allow him. This is why we must stay totally connected and linked up with Christ, who will consume us with good thoughts and keep us far away from those things and people, who have the potential to cause us to sin. As 2 Samuel 2:26 tells us, we must tell the people to stop chasing your brothers, that's not cool Abner and Joab. Must the sword kill forever?

We are told in 1 Samuel 24 how David, who could have killed his enemy Saul, simply chose to cut off a corner of his robe, as he knew the importance of not touching even a hair of God's anointed and doing God's prophet no harm. Even when David's men wanted David to let the blood be on their hands and to take revenge, David said, 'Absolutely not.' When Saul learned of David coming close enough to him to take his life, but choosing not to do so, even Saul, the enemy, sang David's praise as he told him you have done well by me, but I have acted foolishly towards you. Saul even confirms what God had already promised David, which was that David would become King, having a well-established Kingdom. Isn't that good news, that when we do right by our enemies and love them despite their hate towards us, God will reward our obedience and elevate us even more? The Bible cannot lie, as it tells us in Proverbs 16:7 that when God approves of your life, even your enemies will end up shaking your hand. The heart of the King is certainly in the Master's hands.

For the salt throwers, I am so grateful that God's children's success is not built based on what others think about us or what others seek out to do to us, but what God says about us and the doors God flies open for us. MAKE A LIST OF WHAT GOD SAYS ABOUT YOU AND DWELL ON IT REGULARLY…

_____

_____

_____

_____

_____

_____

_____

_____

Now that you have jotted down what the Lord declares about you, affirm yourself daily with the above list, as well as with the promises of God. Declare them over your life daily and let that be your daily affirmation. We do not have to create any affirmations because God already has a lot to say about us in His word and it is all good. One you must list, in order to overcome the salt throwers, is Psalm 41:11, which tells us that when God is pleased with us, our enemies will not triumph over us. Do you believe that? So don't throw salt and don't fret over salt throwers because God will provide an umbrella for you. You are covered, my sister.

In ridding the saltiness and becoming the salt that we were made to be, we must ask God to purify and sanctify our hearts, minds, and tongues. Is it possible to sit at the juror's seat, at the judge's seat, and in the audience? I don't think so. You are either for me or against me and in actuality, if you are against me, you are really against God. Jesus says, if you aren't against Me then you are for Me, if you aren't for Me, then guess what? You are against Me. There is no in-between. Which are you? Romans 14:13 reminds us not to judge and not to put stumbling blocks in a brother's way. Numbers 35 even goes so far as to tell us that even when one does wrong, we ought to be of comfort to them, speaking words that will draw them near to Christ.

Don't throw the rock and hide your hand. Don't stress the petty and don't be petty! Focus on being one of wisdom, directed by God, for God, because it's all about God. How can we sit down with the Father, whom we haven't seen, but we never sit with our earthly father, mother, and our brothers and sisters, whom we see daily? You are the salt of the earth; therefore, strive to be the enhancer of your relationship with others. Don't allow others to make you lose the flavor God has placed in you. You are in control of how you use your salt; hence, use it for the purpose God designed.

14

Might You Be a Miriam

When God is with us, even our enemies will shake our hands and oftentimes, we find that our enemy ends up being blessed by us. Miriam is a perfect example. Miriam teaches us how we should not live in the negative, but in the positive, lest we may be afflicted with a form of leprosy. Might I suggest to you, my sister, that leprosy does not always come in the form of a skin disorder. You may find lesions on your time, your talent, your finances, and your health, that keep things in your life from going smoothly, causing a bumpy life journey. Leprosy can also come in the form of dryness. Maybe your family is going through a dry season that is crusty and oozing out all manner of discord. Could it be the dry season won't end, because in 2 Chronicles 11:4, the Lord says, "We must not go to war against our brothers?" Miriam came against her brother, Moses, and God made her bumpy, crusty, oozy, and isolated. We must not be in the habit of "I gotta say something," because you absolutely do NOT have to say anything. We are told in God's word, to be silent before the Lord. But when we go against that which God is in control of and that which God has ordained, of whom God has set in place to carry out His ministry to His people, we tread on dangerous waters without a boat or a paddle. We leave ourselves wide open with no flotation device in sight. This is like playing with fire. We can't hate and throw salt because someone else has a gift that we want or think we too should have. That's between you and God. Talk to the Gift Giver about it rather than getting salty with the giftee. Haters work behind closed doors, while giftees keep walking into all the doors God is opening.

I asked earlier in the book, who's at your table? The more I think about it, you don't have to invite the enemy to the table. He or she tends to just show up; but one thing about it, God will prepare that table right in front of the enemy, with China, silver and gold utensils, as well as antique décor, etc., all while your enemies sit there and look on. Who is the enemy, one might ask? Isaiah 26:10 gives a good description of the enemy. Check it out. Does this sound like you, or just someone you know? If it sounds like you, then you just might be a Miriam.

Is your spirit contagious? Do you tend to throw a toddler-like tantrum with your friends, coworkers, and family? Do you tend to have a manipulative spirit, critical spirit, and/or complaining spirit? If the answer is yes, you, my friend, just might be a Miriam. A spirit as such is a satanic spirit. It is a spirit controlled and directed by the enemy himself, as Satan wants you to look like him and act like him. He desires to have you defeated, destroyed, distracted, depressed, depleted, doubtful and much more. He wants all of you; but God is not going to play tug-a-war with Satan. God says, whosoever will let him come. You have an opportunity to come just as you are, satanic and all, as God wants to change you. He won't force His way in, but He will stand at the door and knock. It is your choice to let Him in.

15

Understanding the Miriams

I call the Miriams around me "Why, Why, Whyners." Always asking the question, "Why, why, why?" There are some people, who feel because they haven't accomplished certain things in life, it is their goal, their business, their duty to try to halt the progression of others. Some use their shortcomings in attempt to trip up others. Oh Miriams, have you ever thought about the fact that my successfulness comes as a result of my servanthood commitment? We are not in competition, Aaron and Miriam. We are running a race so that we all make it to the finish line. The race isn't given to the swift nor the strong, but to the one who endures until the end. Why Miriam do you feel the need to defeat, shame, and beat me? I am not competing with you, for there is an enemy to be defeated and that enemy 'ain't' you. We wrestle not against one another in the physical, skin for skin, blow for blow, but we wrestle against spiritual wickedness in high places.

Many who act out of foolishness and evilness have an internal wound that is festering; and as they hurt, they seek to hurt others. They seek to strip the favor of God from others; but can I tell you, God isn't having it, because He does not play about His children. No one can steal your joy and no one can take your anointing nor the favor of God that is intended for you. Understand and identify the Miriams in your life and like Christ told Peter, don't be afraid to tell the Miriams in your life to get behind me Satan, even if it means checking your frenemies. If your circle of friends will not support you in your righteousness, or correct you in your unrighteousness, or they are not growing you, building you up, encouraging you, inspiring you, uplifting and praying for you, might you need to do a service check on your circle. It is likely time for an oil change, maintenance, and check-up. Choose your friends wisely and do not be afraid to shake lose the Miriams identified in your circle.

If you are typically not one to choose your friends wisely, might I suggest you keep some Abishais around. There is a difference. I have already hipped you to the Miriams but let me introduce you to the ones you would want in your corner in 1 Samuel 26. First of all, in this passage of scripture we see that David is running for his life. Saul is after him and seeking to murder him. You read it right, Saul wants David g-o-n-e, Gone! David asks, "Is there anyone who will go with me?" Abishai, without hesitancy, answers, "I will go." Now that's a friend - one who will lay down their life for you, one who knows you are in much trouble but does not waver, and one who sticks still ever close to thee. When David and Abishai made it to the camp where Saul and his men were sleeping, Abishai was ready to go in on the enemy. Abishai said, "I will pin him to the ground where he now sleepeth," but David said, "Oh no, God will handle him; I dare not touch God's anointed."

Ladies, I say to you, don't worry about your frenemies. You do not have to try to get them back, get them told nor get them straight. If

God can make rough places smooth and can make crooked places straight, you best believe He can and will handle your frenemies accordingly, and He just may do it while you are watching.

Be sure to surround yourself with people like Barnabas, those who will encourage you, support you, and push you on to doing great things in Christ. I had to throw Barnabas in because though Abishai may be a name that does not ring a bell to you, we all have heard of Barnabas in the Bible, also known as, 'The Encourager.' Ladies, I challenge you not to focus on the Miriams, the questioners, the naysayers, and what-iffers, but I charge you to be the encourager in your circle of friends, like Barnabas. Be the ride or die in your friend group like Abishai, who is willing to stand up and go. Ultimately, strive to be like Christ, having His mind in all things.

16

Rule Makers, Progress Haters

After discussing Miriam, I cannot help but think about a man by the name of Elymus. It is important that I point out some things to note about this man, because oftentimes we hear about the Aarons, the Miriams, the Pharoah - 'Let my people go' episodes; however, there are many other people in the Bible who serve as evidence that God will not allow any man, woman, boy, or girl to halt the ministry work of His kingdom from going forth. You see there was a 'prudent man' in Acts 13 who wanted to hear a word from the Lord; hence, he called for Barnabas and Paul. Elymus, in his demonic uptake, decided he would deter the 'prudent man' from hearing from God. Paul looked Elymus dead in his eyes and called him out for who he really was - a child of the devil and one against righteousness. Paul declared unto him that he would be stricken with blindness, which he was. Hence, the 'prudent man' in astonishment, believed in God who had sent the brethren. 'Oh, be careful little mouth what you say,' is an understatement in this case, because it truly cost Elymus 20/20, as his sight was dimmed, and he required someone to guide him.

God does not play about His word and He does not play about His prophets. As a pastor's daughter and now a pastor's wife, trust me, I have seen the 'Do my prophet no harm' statement go live and in action and it is a very scary sight to see. It has me scared to disagree at times with my own husband, who is also my pastor, because I realize, 'God ain't playing around.' He says what He means and He means what He says, PERIODTTT! Ask Elymus, who was blinded as a result of his baseness.

A king and leader who teaches one thing but does another is often referred to as a hypocrite, best defined as one who emphasizes rules for others to follow, yet does not follow them himself. Sound familiar? The Bible calls them Pharisees and Sadd-u-cees. What do you call them _____? I am sure that one blank would not be enough to list the many Miriams, Pharisees, Sadducees, and hypocrites that you have faced in this life. You know the list would be quite long and lengthy if we really started listing those who have been critical of, questioned, and murmured against that which God told us to do, as if we are to follow the commands of them, instead of hearing from and following God. Luke 11:28 tells us we are blessed when we not only hear the word of God but when we obey it.

So, let me get this right, "You, Miriam, expect me to go totally against God to follow what you think I ought to be doing in and with the gift that God has given me, whether it's the gift of prophesy, the gift of evangelism, the gift of hospitality, the gift of administration or whatever gift God has so graciously gifted me to use in His service and for His glory? Why would you feel compelled to hate on my blessedness, when God has clearly said, whosoever will let Him come?" God has something for all of us to do. He is a giving God. Put that hater energy into having a talk with

Jesus and allowing Him to speak to you that which He has for you to do. You see God called people with the latter spirit, the Pharisees that is, "foolish," as those who worked to make tombs for the prophets.

As I mentioned previously, I will be the first to warn folk, "That is not what you want to do. Trust me!" I have seen God work, and what I will say, is that God will not always touch you as He touched Miriam. You may not be put out of the tent, or rather put down on your sick bed, but He may just decide to touch someone close to you; and that, many times, is harder to watch than being afflicted yourself. Your loved one going through, as a result of your ignorance, is not what any of us would choose. So, it's easier on all to just take heed to the word of God through God's chosen, anointed, and appointed, and follow the vision given for the people of God. His sheep hear His voice and follow Him.

In the Old Testament, the people never saw the Lord; but they simply heard His voice and they followed. When they didn't hear His voice, as it frightened them to hear His voice, they would hear Him speaking through the man of God. How many times do we hear and read in the Bible, "This is the word from the Lord, follow, and obey everything I have commanded?" Why did He keep repeating it? Because He knew we were a stubborn, rebellious, disobedient, whining, complaining, critical group of Miriams on repeat. Yes! Set to rewind!

You do not have to give in to and address the critical spirits, because God will handle the haters. In this walk with Christ, you will have haters, enemies, and those who simply do not like you because of the God you serve and how the Lord has seen fit to bless you and your family. Look at Paul and Silas - thrown in jail for preaching Christ. Everybody is not going to like you in your witnessing to them about Christ. They will call you 'goody-two-shoes,' 'smarty-pants,' or 'holier than thou,' but that's okay, you keep preaching, speaking, and ministering to the masses. Jeremiah 26 tells us in other words, don't shoot the messenger. The people tried to kill Jeremiah when he was simply saying what doth saith the Lord. Change your lives, do what's right, and God will change His mind on bringing disaster and destroying the temple.

We find in 1 King 5 where David didn't get to build the temple because people were fighting him. He had many enemies to defeat before building the temple; so, God said, you know what, don't worry about it, I will make your son Solomon King and he will build the temple to worship me. God's plan cannot be stopped. David had to defeat enemies for the will of God to go forth as planned. Pastors may have to bury some folk, have some funerals, and visit some hospitals before being able to carry out what doth saith the Lord. Either way, God's plan will prevail.

Gravity weighs down, pulls, and tugs on you, much like a stronghold and a hater. In Luke 11:23, we are told, if you are not working with me, you are working against me. Every kingdom that fights against itself will break apart. Would you not say that is what we are facing now, Oh America? Evil spirits will come to stay, that is, if you don't put them out. And even when they leave, as stated before, evil spirits will trust to leave and return with seven more evil friends, if you entertain them and fail to stop them in their tracks. Miriam was put out of the tent. Separate yourself from the Miriams in your life, those of whom cannot find anything good to say and are always critical, always murmuring, or as my dad says, always trying to take a slice of bread out of your mouth while God is steady backing a truckload of bread in your driveway. God will prepare the table before you in the presence of your enemies, so keep it moving as Moses did in the midst of Sister Miriam. Where God is taking you, they ain't ready, so put 'em out your tent! Psalm 78 speaks of rebellious, murmuring, and complaining people - those who see all of what God is doing, yet are still unsatisfied. Be ye not as these, for this is not in any way pleasing to God.

17

The Word of God Is Sharper – Keep It Handy

As we go through life, we find it easier to tell someone off than to turn the other cheek. We find it more fulfilling to have the last word than to keep still, keep quiet, and let God fight our battles. Have you a Judas in your camp - a traitor - all about the money bag and one who will sell you out? We all have at some point or another. If not a Judas, maybe you have a Peter in your circle. They speak good talk; they say they love you and will die with or for you but deny you when the real test presents itself. But don't you worry about the Peters and those like Judas. Simply speak as Jesus spoke, "Get thee behind me Satan." Don't you try to get back at them. God will divide (scatter), defeat (conquer), and devour (destroy), the very one who is trying to attack and deter you from carrying out the ministry of Christ.

We may find it more convenient to take revenge than to wait on God to repay, but let me assure you, He will repay. I have seen Him work. Learn to pray for your enemies and be kind to them, as difficult as it might be. Mark 14 tells us about the ones who in secret wanted to take Jesus out.

There are some in secret who want to take you out also. Don't be fooled by the words they speak, the smiles, the hugs, the love songs, and their hanging close to you. Some of the very ones that sought to take Jesus out were some of the very ones hanging close to Him, checking out His every move. Jesus said you all came at me with swords and clubs as if I were a criminal, after all I have done for you. Some of the same people who smile in your face, who have eaten at the table with you, who you have entertained at your home are some of the same people who will either overlook you or come for you in the most conniving, wicked, and scheming way. You recall Freddy, don't you? One, two, they are coming for you. Three, four, you better shut that door, and lock it! Don't ignore the situation like you don't see them, but also do not go into attack mode on them. Simply pray for them. Some folks you spent time with, funeralized their loved ones, prayed some back to restoration, will be the very ones to flee the scene and desert you in your weakest moments. Some of these very people will try to bring accusations against you, say all manner of evil against you, and question you on things they already know have no substance; but, yet and still, Jesus said not a word. Everything, my sister, does not deserve a response. Pray, keep calm, and take a deep breath. God's got it.

    We must know, it is necessary that we go through these things, as Jesus said, "So that the scriptures come true and for your growth," as the Lord builds us in these situations. We must be merciful if we expect God to be merciful to us. I have learned through the years to fight not by my own might but by the power of God that worketh in me. This is why it is so important to know the word, and to hide the word in our hearts, so that it will come back to our remembrance when we need it most. I don't have to make anything up or come up with my own words to combat or diffuse a situation, because God's word is hidden in my heart and it can conquer, heal, deliver, set free, and pierce even down to the bone and marrow.

Have you ever seen people in your neighborhood walking for daily exercise with a stick in their hand? Be it a broom, a golf club, a mop handle, or just a stick that they have found. We all have seen this in our lifetime and it's pretty normal. I mean we understand if an animal attempted to attack them, they would defend themselves. Question, have you ever seen this same image; however, with a belt? A flimsy belt, really?! How can an individual defend oneself from a vicious animal with something as flimsy as a belt? First of all, the animal would have to get extremely close to them and secondly, the belt is likely to be a little more difficult to manage and strike with. Let me bring this closer to home. A flimsy saint will have it difficult trying to win the battle, because with every swing they will flip, flop, bend, and miss their target. However, a golf club and stick carrying saint, one who is prepared, one who has on the proper armor to defeat the enemy head on, one who is ready for battle and can sing, "Come what may from day to day, God will take care of me," will be able to handle his or her own.

I am reminded in the story of Job, that no matter what comes our way, to always trust in God, because with Him comes a double portion. Things may appear one way, but they get 'gooder and gooder' (better and better for the sake of my English teacher), and He gets sweeter and sweeter as the days go by. The truth of the matter is that many of us trust the chairs we sit in, the line in the middle of the roadway, that friend, or that hairdresser (because you know we don't just let anybody do our hair), and even our own strength over trusting God at His word. God's word speaks so much strength and power to our weary souls. I stay in His word because it strengthens me when I am weak and it makes me stronger even when I feel like I am doing pretty alright. I need it every day and every hour because I know that as I stay in His Word, I stay close to Him. God's word reminds me that He has broken the teeth of the wicked; hence, I am determined not to fret due to evildoers.

Psalm 53:5 goes so far as to let us know that God will even scatter the bones of our enemies. Visualize your enemies discombobulated - totally confused and destroyed by the hand of God. The word of God has a way of confusing the enemy and cutting down to the bone and marrow, as I cannot stress enough. When God is for you, who can be against you?

In Acts 4, we find Peter and John courageously speaking what doth saith the Lord amongst people who were haters. Seeing their courage and the fact these men were not educated, they could tell that they had been in the presence of Jesus. Ladies, when we spend time in the presence of Jesus, degrees do not matter, as people can see the favor of God all over us. As we spend time with God and in the word of God, it truly makes a difference even in the haters around us, as we have the power to change minds and lives by the Lord God who worketh in us.

Help us Lord to speak and declare Your word with boldness and without fear. Fill us up with Your Holy Spirit that we may stand against the wiles of the evil one with Your word, not ours. Amen!

18

You Are the Salt of the World, Taste Like It

What reflection do people see when they see you? Many people look for validation in all the wrong places. Some look to the lost world, which reflects as dark pepper; however, we need to be as the salt mixed in with the pepper, that which stands out amongst the darkness, amongst the dark and evil world. In the world but not of the world.

When I think about being the salt of the earth, I can't help but think about Matthew 13 and the planting of the seeds. As I read about the various seeds, I am reminded of what a stubborn breed we are at times. We are often closed-eared, closed-minded, and though we attend church service after church service, we seem to still be far from Thee, as the seed often falls on all kinds of ground, but fertile ground.

Jeremiah 31 tells us to Sing, Shout, Praise, Be Happy, and Have Joy. Why? Because There is Hope! Hence, we should look like hope, act like hope, live like hope, walk like hope, talk like hope, endure like hope, be wrapped up and embraced in hope, because in God there is hope! We must look like Whose we are. We are God's; we are chosen; we are loved;

we are absolutely amazing; we are a miracle; we are God's own predestined and creative projection to greatness; we are what God says we are; therefore, we must act like it, be like it, and taste like it. Oh, taste and see that God is great and greatly to be praised; and because of God's goodness and greatness - I being of Him, born as an heir and joint-heir, a sibling to His Son, Jesus - I too, am destined for greatness.

In 1 Chronicles 4, we learn of the Prayer of Jabez. "Lord, increase my territory," Jabez inquired of God. In this prayer, we often get so caught up in the increase that all we see is God giving us more of this and more of that, totally missing the sincere prayer in Jabez's heart that God would increase him above and out of the way of his enemies so that his enemies would not hurt or harm him. Often, we miss the part where Jabez begs of God to stay with him - which God answered. Often, we want to focus on the increase without the 'Stay with me Jesus' part or better yet, 'Lord, keep me with You.' We often get so wrapped up in the increase that we fail to plead the blood of Jesus over ourselves, family, and friends because we are so busy trying to get more, more, and more. If we aren't daily praying for covering, covering, and covering, we will not enjoy the increase that is to be granted.

In being the salt of the earth, we at some point have to shift our mindset from being caught up in ourselves as a taste tester, one who wants to be served by everyone else, instead of being the one serving. We love to try samples and many of us can get completely full off of sampling from many different tables; but God desires us to be the sample and the example, so that others may taste and see Jesus in us, as we are the salt of the earth. Before COVID, we would take our kids to the mall after Sunday service and sample the various food establishments, which offered samples. The kids loved it, because by the time we finished sampling a little bit of this and a little bit of that, we would be full, which meant, when we finally decided which restaurant we would order a meal from, we had plenty to take home for later. Ladies, God doesn't want us dipping in this place and that place and eating from this table and that table because when we fill up on all this stuff that the world is trying to give us to sample, we leave no room for God. If we truly desire God to fill us up, we must empty ourselves of some stuff. We must ask God to clean our heart of jealousy, pride, selfishness, greed, malice, lies, and anything that is not like Him. God wants all of us, not just some, and He wants to be breakfast, lunch, and dinner, not seconds. He wants to be our main course, for He is our Daily Bread and our Bread of Life; and we wash it all down with the Living Water, quenching and fulfilling our every need, hunger, and thirst.

When I was younger, my mom was a home economics teacher for special needs students, which meant, she would practice on my brother and me, by baking cakes and goodies that she would plan on preparing with her students the following week. We were treated with the pre-planning of her baking classes by being able to taste all the goodies as her taste testers. Mom would always give my brother and me the leftover batter and even the stirrer from the blender to enjoy as we waited for the cake to be made. My mother would leave a good bit of batter in the bowl for us to enjoy and she would sacrifice eating any in order to leave enough for my brother and me. What a selfless act of love! Now mind you, this was all before we realized that the raw egg in the mixture could have potentially killed us, like took us out y'all! But, the fact of the matter is, we are still here, thank you Jesus; and it tasted really good. Mom could have decided to just eat that good-tasting batter herself and not share any with us, but she did not. She thought enough of my brother and me to treat us to that great tasting batter, even before the cake itself was ready. That's love!

God expects the same of us, as the salt of the earth. He expects us to share His love with others that they will taste the salt within us, taste the goodness of Christ which dwells in us, taste the greatness that lies within us, and taste and see His glory shone round about us. He does not want us to keep it all to ourselves but to share His love with others.

My sisters, and my brothers (who may also be reading this book), if others are not tasting the salt of Christ in you, if you aren't sharing the good stuff - the good news of Jesus, with others, then might I suggest you are being selfish. If something tastes good, if you find a new recipe, if you find the bomb restaurant, and happen to just run up on a terrific dish, you are going to run and tell that. So, why not run and tell the good news of Jesus Christ? Why not run and tell about the Chef of all Chefs, who feeds the hungry, the well-fed, and the ones who don't have sense enough to realize they are starving? Why not tell of God's great recipe, of how He died for our sins, was buried, and rose again on the third day, according to the scriptures? Share the recipe of Christ, who was beaten like dough, placed in a tomb like an oven, rose like yeast, and tastes like Pillsbury, but even better. Tell the world, saints; and listen up for those reading this book who may be a sinner, "OH, TASTE AND SEE THAT THE LORD IS GOOD; HE IS GOOD, HE IS GOOD, HE IS GOOD!"

Now shifting gears a little here, Paul was amongst some wishy-washy folk, as one might say, who one minute were kind and gracious to him; however, when a snake jumped on him and took hold of his hand, the people turned their thoughts about him, stating, "He must be a murderer." After they witnessed and tasted the salt of Jesus coming through him, seeing that he did not die, they quickly changed their minds and thought, oh, well maybe he's just a god. Be the salt of the earth and others can't help but know that there is a power greater than you that worketh in you. Even when they can't taste the salt in you, they will see it and know it is there, like a good ole' salty and buttery pretzel from the Pretzel Company or those Mickey D fries which are glistening with big ole' huge flakes of salt.

As I end this chapter, let me share with you that you won't always feel like salt, because some days you will truly feel like a nut, remember the nut and crumbs I mentioned earlier. I am just being honest. There are many days and even many moments throughout a 24-hour day that I, like David, have to encourage myself in the Lord, because I feel like I am so overwhelmed and have so much to do and so much going on around me that I totally feel lost and hollow, like a hollow nutshell. But I am reminded that even in the dry places of the desert where David had to hide from Saul, God protected him and kept him out of harm's way.

Ladies, in being the salt of the earth, there are some days you will feel dried out; but might I suggest to you that God sometimes takes us through some very dry places to protect us and keep us safe from the death valley. I mean who wouldn't choose dry over death, any day? Had David come out of the darkness and dryness inside the cave and gone into the daylight before God instructed him to, he would have potentially lost his life. Know that even in the dark, dry moments and stages of life, God is protecting us, and in due time, in God's time, the morning will come. God will expose us in the daylight so that His glory will shine through us; and although we are seen, the enemy can't touch us. Don't curse the cave moments but grow closer to God in them and keen your ears to God's voice, that you may clearly hear His next steps for you, because if you come out in the daylight before God's timing, the Sauls in your life may attack and try to take you out. Your time to shine will come. Trust God for it and remember in your shining, it's not about you but it's all about Christ, who shineth in you. In your desert moments, please believe that God will do a 1 Samuel 23:26 on you. He will have you going along one side of the mountain and the enemy will be on the other side; but even though it may seem like the enemy is closing in on you, God will protect you - being the salt of the earth that you are.

Have you ever wondered why when an ice storm is approaching, the city pours salt on the road? Salt has a way of preventing the freezing over or refreezing of ice on the road, which could potentially cause accidents, destruction, and tragedy. As the salt of the earth, God has put something inside all of us to prevent our own destruction, to protect ourselves and others from slippery, sloping accidents that could potentially be prevented, and ultimately to be the salt that glistens and not that which flies. So be the salt, don't throw it. God wants the best for us, and He expects us to give our best to Him and do our best for others. Be the salt of the earth, my sisters, because that is who you are!

PART FOUR

P8TIENTLY AWAITING

As humans, we are a very impatient species. Let's just admit it. Many of us can think back to a time, in which we felt God was taking too long, that is if we even consulted with God. Many go ahead of God or bypass God altogether, one or the other, and then sit in a pit or end up in a valley as a result. One thing we, as humans, do way too often is share our problems and even our goals with others who can either care less, cannot do anything about it, or who will try to halt our progress. You do realize everyone that says they are for you aren't necessarily for you, right? I pray for the spirit of discernment daily, and I would suggest you do the same because it is a sure way to show up those who do not mean you any good. But that's another topic for another book.

My brothers and sisters, as you wait on Christ to 'Do what He does,' might I recommend you not share your problems on all these social media platforms to all these folk that cannot do anything to help you. It is a waste of time, and I don't know about you, but my time is precious. Take it to Jesus. Tell God all about your problems, your goals, your hopes, and your dreams. I mean He knows all about you and He is the one who can help you and see you through successfully. Know this, some people thrive from seeing others suffer or seeing others beneath them. Learn to patiently wait on Jesus!

Might I also suggest that as we wait, we should choose to BE GRATEFUL, NOT HATEFUL. I know many of us have been in a waiting room, waiting for the nurse to call us back to the room or waiting on our vehicle to get fixed. In our waiting, and we all are guilty, if we feel the wait is taking too long or others are being called before us, we will get an attitude with the staff; and they may have some explaining to do. Yeah, that may work in this world, but it doesn't work like that with Christ. As we wait for Christ to perform what He has already said in His word that He will perform, we must patiently wait and trust that God is going to do what He said He's going to do. Now, don't get me wrong, you can keep going back to the desk and inquiring, or in other words, keep falling on your knees and inquiring of God, keep talking to Him, keep blessing and praising His holy name, but don't start cursing the God who blesses you because you aren't getting what you want when you want it. Praise God in advance. Praise God while still in shackles and watch Him send an earthquake to break the chains. Don't believe it? Ask Rhoda, the little girl, and those in the prayer house the night that Paul and Silas were freed from the chains of bondage; better yet, ask Paul and Silas themselves, who at midnight were praying, singing, and praising God. In Isaiah 45:2, God says He will break down gates of bronze and cut through bars of iron just for you. He will go before us and level out an entire mountain. Isn't that good news?

In our most down moments, I have found that many people say prayer is the farthest thing from their minds because they just don't feel like praying or think that it will not change anything. But I beg to differ, as prayer is the closest thing to you that you can do and get results because prayer still works and prayer changes things, situations, minds, and hearts. We, my brothers and sisters, have to learn how to Pray, Sing, and Praise God even in our **WAITING ON GOD TO PERFORM** what He said He would do.

Psalm 107 tells us that although they got into trouble, and they suffered misery, God always came to their rescue, which serves as a fact that God will come to see about us. So be not dismayed. The good people will be happy and rejoice as we are lifted out of our affliction and God begins to move on our behalf, but the wicked will say nothing. Be mindful of the 'Do-nothings and the say-nothings.' When the onlookers look on and have nothing to say, just know you likely will not win the praise of the wicked, only the good. Press on anyhow. God is working, while they are watching.

19

Waiting P8tiently for the Winning Season

With a family full of boys, there is always some type of sports competition going on. Whether basketball or football, there is always an opportunity for someone to win something. One thing we always stress to our boys is that in a competition, there is always an opponent; and the opponent is not on your team. We remind them to ensure they have identified who the opponent is, the color the opponent has on, and know what the opponent looks like so that they do not turn on their teammate and begin going against the wrong someone. In order to win, you have to work with the coach, as well as the team, and not treat them as if they are the opponent. We get it all wrong when we stop fighting the opponent and begin fighting our teammates. In healthcare, we call this an autoimmune disease. This is when the body stops working with itself and begins fighting against itself. A body that attacks itself makes it hard to win. Matthew 12:30 tells us, if you aren't for me, then you are against me. As noted previously, if you aren't working with me, then it's pretty obvious you are working against me. Isn't that the truth?

Ladies, we have a real enemy to fight and a real battle to defend; hence, we are reminded in 1 Samuel 17:47, "The battle belongs to the Lord." Whatever your giant, your difficulty, your lack thereof might be, please understand this day, that you have a God who can defeat any enemy, any opponent, any opposition you face in this life. When I was in high school, I joined the track team. Yes, I joined the track team - you read it right! For those who know me, go ahead and laugh because I just got tickled at myself all over again. What was I thinking? I had no intentions of winning anything because, in actuality, I did not even know how to run. The reason I joined the track team is that it appeared they were always getting a chance to miss school and go to track meets. That sounded like something that was right down my alley. Miss school and meet others on the track, oh yeah, why not, so I thought! That was until I got out there and started running. I, the non-runner, with others who were true-runners, quickly realized that my breath was left back around that 30-second mark, because listen, by the time I made it to the finish line, as likely number eight out of eight, I felt like I needed oxygen and IV fluids. I was fit to be tied! I ran one race and that was enough for me to know, ummm being in school is not that bad after all. Consequently, I quit. Yes, I quit! But if I can pull any lesson learned out of that to share with you, I would say, ensure you are on the right field for the winning season. I would also note, it is important that you are a team player and are contributing to the team and not pulling the team down. Whew! Let me just hit repeat on that one. Ensure you are on the right field, playing the right sport, being a team player if you are to declare a winning season. What am I saying, one might ask? Running track was not my thing, not at all - far from it! Being in the classroom was, as I was an 'A' Honor Roll student. If I had decided to keep running track, my winning season likely would have never come, because I was somewhere that God had not told me to be, trying to win a race that God had not given me clearance to run. Now, say all of what you just read again and let that settle.

In this life, we must be intentional in our waiting season. Are we in the right place, at the right time, to receive the blessing that God has in store for us? Are we at the well in the heat of the day? Are we positioned just right in the crowd to where we can press, reach out, and touch the hem of His garment, that we might be made whole, and be healed of the issue of blood, overcoming the issues of life? Are we sitting in the tree positioned on just the right branch, you Zacchaeus you, to see Jesus with our own eyes? Are we in the temple praying for quite some time, maybe even decades, you Annas, awaiting the coming of the Messiah? In our waiting, we must ensure we are positioned on the right playing field so that we do not miss out on our winning season, doing stuff and more stuff, and all kinds of busy, busy stuff, that God has not told us to do.

In your waiting, trust God! He's 'The Man' with the master plan! In Matthew 10:31, we are reminded that we are worth more than a sparrow. God values every one of us on a personal level; and He expects us to win, by the power of Christ Jesus who worketh in us. We are More than Conquerors. We will win!

20

P8tiently Overcoming Distractions

We have all faced opposition and distractions at some point in our lives. I am reminded of the many distractions Paul faced as he carried out the work of the Lord. In Acts 18, the Jews openly came against Paul, but we find Paul not giving in or giving up, not throwing in the towel, not bending, but pressing on towards the mark of the prize of the high calling, which is in Christ Jesus. The devil would love to stop us dead in our tracks on our mission for Christ, but we cannot let distractions stop us. As Paul, we too must shake off the dust and keep it moving. Paul tells the people 'I done tried to told ya so,' LOL! In other words, Paul says your blood will be on your heads and it ain't my fault! Periodttt! Might I add, this passage of scripture also teaches me the importance of knowing when the distraction is not others but merely ourselves or our unbeknownst of, under learning, or inability to know when to move past and move on. Later in this same passage of scripture, I love how Priscilla and Aquilla saw something in Apollos; so, they took him to better prepare, better equip, and better educate him. Apollos was missing a key component of the gospel, so this husband-and-wife team helped school him. Don't allow what you don't know to hold you back from conquering what is yours to conquer. Apollos took notice of what he had learned and went on to Achaia to further spread the gospel of Jesus Christ. He didn't waver, he didn't stop, he was not offended, but he took what he learned and rocked with it. He was encouraged by the brothers and sisters, and he was not afraid to go against opposition from the Jews to prove that Jesus was indeed the Messiah. Opposition, my sisters, is a distraction, but you can overcome it.

Ladies, don't sit on the fact that you may not know all of what you think you should know about a certain something. Simply start moving in it with boldness and courage and watch God reward your willingness to move past the 'I don't know' distractions. Learn as you go, become aware as you go, but whatever you do, do not let the hurdles of the unknown scare you into fear that blocks you from moving past the unknown. The anticipation is most times scarier than real time. Working in the school system, as the summer months approach a close in July, I have always felt a cry, a whole scrunched-up face type of breakdown coming on. The closer it gets to August; the more anxiety comes. But then, on the first day of school, it is like the anxiety miraculously disappears, never to return until the next long break. Educators who are reading this can likely relate and agree that the anticipation is always worse than the actual going back. Hence, don't let the anticipation and anxiety get the best of you and distract you from God's plan for you, but be reminded that God has told us to be anxious for nothing but in everything by prayer and supplication, with thanksgiving, make our requests known unto Him.

In 2 Kings 13:5, after many years of the people of Israel suffering at the hands of the king of Aram, the Lord provides a deliverer to save the people of Israel. My sister, in your waiting season, don't curse the suffering that you may be experiencing because God has planned a way of escape and He will deliver you from that which may have you feeling depressed, oppressed, and regressed. In this life, we will face obstacles, just like we face on the interstate. Construction, detours, and delays, but we must not get so focused on the delays or what I like to call distractions, that we totally forget about our destination. In other words, don't turn around and go back to the house, just because you will be late getting to your destination, due to delays. Push through, sit patiently, or take the back roads, but first consult your GPS, because the back roads may be crowded as well with people who are looking for a bypass route. OMG, I must say myself, that's good if we would only apply it to our spiritual lives. First things first, before leaving the house, one who is prepared will check the GPS before heading to one's destination. Talk to Jesus! A prepared saint wants direction from God because talking to God about it first may prevent you from running into that accident on the interstate, that roadblock, or that construction site. Just like checking the GPS first may guide you around the road construction and help you know what time to leave home to make it to your destination on time, consulting Christ before doing anything, will do the same for you.

By talking to God about any and every action we take, we can prevent delays and likely get to our destination sooner than planned, being directed around roadblocks. If a railroad arm comes down, do we stop, or do we go around it, potentially killing ourselves and those in the car with us? Or do we take it as a sign from the engineer that danger lurks if we should go over this track while the arm is down? Same with Christ, sometimes He has put the stop arm down to remind us to wait because it's not time yet - just wait. We see the red lights flashing, and still we find some kind of way to proceed around it with an oncoming train headed straight toward us. Destruction awaits us just around the corner, on the tracks, and past the stop arm that God has placed before us for a reason. God says in Psalm 91 that He will give His angels charge concerning us, to go ahead of us and to guard us in all our ways; so why would you want to run ahead instead of patiently awaiting what God is going to do? Stop rushing God. He doesn't rush us! He gives us 24 hours a day, seven days a week, 365 days in a year, and chance after chance. He patiently awaits us to come to Him, even when we put Him on the back burner, He's still there! Don't rush God, but 'P8tiently Await' what He is doing because His time is much better than anything that we can ask or think.

My sisters, distractions often come from the dark places of life, as Psalm 11:2 mentions darts, which are fixated on us, ready to shoot at any time those who are genuine and honest. But don't you be distracted. Stay the course and patiently await the Father to rescue you in your time of need. What we need to overcome distractions are right at our fingertips, in fact, as God told Moses, it's in your hand. What's in your hand? Whatever God has placed in your hand, whether a stick or whatever it may be, please do not discount it. God can build a fire with the stick in your hand. Give Him what you got. Don't discount what God has given you; but use it and watch Him build on it when you give back to Him, what He has given to you. Overlook the distractions, my sister. Your destination is in your hands, specially placed by the Master Himself; so, it's on you to consult the Man with the Master plan and move past the hurdles and distractions in life.

21

P8tiently Overcoming Suffering in Our Waiting

In 2 Kings 13:23, we find that in Israel's suffering, despite anything that they had previously done, the Lord had mercy on them and helped them because of His agreement with Abraham, Isaac, and Jacob. Although they were troubled in Israel, they were not destroyed. Do you realize that God will come to your rescue, as a result of an agreement with your ancestors, your great-grandfather, grandfather, and your father? I know for a fact that I am living on the prayers and the connections of my parents, grandparents, and great-grands, many of whom have gone on before me. It is not of my own that I am not consumed even in my suffering.

In 2 Corinthians 4, we are reminded that although we are troubled and hard-pressed, we cannot bend; we cannot break; we cannot throw in the towel; and we cannot give up. We must stay the course and allow the life of Jesus to give life to the dead situations in our lives, to live through us, and to light up the dark circumstances around us. What seems to be a dead cause, a dead circumstance, a dead situation is only asleep when we put it in the hands of God. What you thought was gone, as a result of your suffering, is only on snooze. I am reminded, not only of the woman with the issue of blood who was made whole as a result of touching the hem of Christ's garment; but I am also reminded of the dead man in 2 Kings 13 who was thrown into the Prophet Elisha's grave. Interestingly, when he touched the man of God's bones, he was brought back to life. My sister, when you get connected, linked up with, and touch others who have been infused, empowered, enhanced, and filled up with the spirit of God, something on the inside will begin to work on the outside. There will be a change that will overcome you, even in your suffering, that will bring back to life that which you thought had departed. In your suffering, be aware of your surroundings and who you are allowing to lay hands on you, who you are allowing in your space, or better yet, whose space you are in, because it could literally be a matter of life or death.

Are you suffering, my sister, due to past regrets that have weighed you down and caused you to be in a place of shame? Are you ashamed of your past and ashamed to speak up about how God can deliver any of us from our past sins? How deep are your roots in Christ? Often, we think our roots are deeper than they actually are, until we hit rock bottom, until our hearts are broken, until we go through life's trying times. I am aware of many people who have had a tree in their yard, which roots were so deep into the ground that they began to spread and take root into the sewer lines in their homes. This created a humongous disaster in their homes, as mess began to back up not only in the toilets but also in their tubs and showers. When we take root in God, I mean really get tied up and tangled up in Him, He will drive the mess out and He will back us up.

Isaiah 43:18 reminds us to forget those things that are in the past. Do not allow Abishais in your circle nor your personal space. These are the ones who like to pull up your past. In 2 Samuel 19, we are reminded of how Abishai tried to throw Shimei under the bus by suggesting he be put to death for what he had done in the past. I know you are likely thinking, "Now, earlier she told us we need some Abishais, but now she is saying to ditch the Abishais." There are bits of Abishai that I would say to take and pieces of Abishai that I would say to leave. In this case, Shimei had come to his senses and was ready to meet the Lord, although his record was one of sinning. All have sinned and come short of the glory of God. If one has not sinned, be ye the first to throw the stone. David responded, "And what does this have to do with you, this ain't your business?" I love me some David because David will tell it just like it is. David stayed correcting Abishai who was always on ready to take a brother out. We are reminded that as others are trying to bury you before God calls you home, God is a keeper, as we find David saved Shimei's life and made an oath with him. Whatever sins were committed in my past or your past, my sister, they are done and over - finished. Do not dwell on the past. Remember always that God has thrown your sins into the sea of forgetfulness, never to return.

When we walk, we walk forward, not looking back at what we just left behind. Memories are there to remind us of where we have come from. Moratoriums are there to stop us in our tracks and leave us in a spot of either nothingness or do somethingness, a place of reflection, a place of planning out the next steps, a place of seeking God for what He desires next for our lives. Movement is taking a clear stance to get up and do something. Do I stay in a place of memories and live in my past, including past hurt, past disappointment, and past pain? Do I stop and suspend everything in the moratorium process and become even the more stagnated by my past and my self-induced doubt and inabilities; or do I look to the hills from which cometh my help and declare I will head to the mountain, where my help, my change, my encounter with God comes from? The latter of which can only occur through movement.

Get up my sister, don't linger in the place where you are. The Bible declares in Psalm 23 that we go through the valley, but we don't dwell in the valley. We dwell in the house of the Lord, in the secret place, in His safety. He shall hide us in His tabernacle, covered in His shadow and He can and will take us places we never thought possible. Overcome, press through, get up, get out, and be the change that you want to see in your home, on your job, in your community, and in the world.

The devil will have you to waddle in your circumstances and stay stagnant, never getting up, never doing, only settling and being mediocre; but God says otherwise. God declares, you are chosen, selected, predestined, anointed, and graced for such a time as this. Therefore, get up Esther, and make your presence known, because when they see you, they will see your Daddy in you. You know how we do, "Girl, you know you look just like your daddy." Declare, "Lord, let me look like You - my Daddy, my Father God." May I have eyes to see what you see in me and others. Lord, let my voice speak what you speak; let my nose smell the array of fragrances of which you so beautifully adorned the earth; let my skin radiantly shine bright that others may follow the light that shineth in me. Jesus, let my cheeks blush with newness of life that You instill in every fiber of our being - restoration, rejuvenation, and innovation to overcome that which has been and press towards that which is to come.

My suffering does not define who I am, it simply expresses where I've come from, provides fuel for where I am going, and ignites the burning desire in me to overcome. I am reminded of the Hebrew slaves and what all they went through. Despite their circumstances, they prospered in their problems, prospered in their purpose, and prospered in their perseverance against all odds and so can you. There is nothing that is too hard for God and nothing good shall He withhold from us! Paul reminds us in Ephesians 3, not to be discouraged, for in our suffering we honor God.

Imagine what all occurred before the beautiful birth of Jesus. Mary went through shame and anguish, and I am sure Joseph went through a time of disappointment and confusion; but after all of that, the joy that came with the birth of Baby Jesus, made an impact on not only them but all who came to see and know Him. There is so much joy on the other side of our suffering, so don't you at any point give up or cave in. Press on and see what the end is going to be, for God has secured your future. Just as God impregnated Mary with Baby Jesus, God will impregnate you with His spirit to rise above your suffering, which comes only for a season.

Ladies, let me remind you that you do not have to look like what you are going through. Think on good things, my sister - things that reveal hope; prosperous things; things that are of a good report. When we think about good things, we look beautiful inside and out; and God is pleased with our insides because He has x-ray vision, 'ya know! In addition, those who come in contact with us are able to witness what is birthed from within to form the beautiful smile and joy we express in our facial tone on the outside. However, when we live a life based upon our suffering, we tend to harp on and look like those things that do not bring about peace and joy, but that of disappointment and discouragement.

Our human instinct outwardly expresses and reflects what is on the inside, so think about good things, not bad. Let's think about the consumption of a lemon. It is very difficult to eat a lemon without tasting the sourness on the inside of your body and reflecting a lemon face on the outside - turned up lip, and sour look. The same happens when we think about things that are sour and not good. If you were to smell something that stinks, your face wrinkles up, frowns up, and your facial expression becomes difficult to look at for those around you. Focus not your mind on unpleasant things but let your mind dwell on things that are good, in hopes of things getting better.

As my husband often preaches, 'You have to see it before you see it.' You must see yourself on the other side of your suffering because it looks better over there, trust me! Regardless of your suffering, beauty comes from within and is revealed on the outside in your character and what others see. Therefore, do not allow your suffering to define who you are because you, my sister, are greater than your suffering.

22

Patiently Pressing Towards Our Ultim8 Goal

Paul suffered many things, but he pressed on; he thanked God in all things; he still rejoiced; he stayed the course; he declared to live is Christ and to die is gain; and he served in whatever capacity God used him in, not making excuses because of the accusers, haters, and criticizers. Paul preached in and out of season, even leaving friends behind to follow Christ. Paul did all the latter plus he found time to motivate, uplift, and encourage the people of God to do the same. Paul encouraged the people to press toward the mark; to not give up; to not turn against each other, but to wait on the Lord and to follow in His ways and calling on their lives. Paul simply wanted to please God!

What is it that you desire? What is it that you have been expecting God for? Is it that nice house, land, a job, a man, or would you say, simply joy, peace of mind, covering from dangers seen and unseen, and to fulfill that which God has called you to, to the best of your ability? Have you stopped long enough to talk to God and He to you, or do you have a habit of hearing from others before and over what you hear from God? Might

I suggest you shut the door, cut the busyness of life, and sit down so that you can talk to God, and He can speak to you.

Back in the day, they used to say, "Slow your role!" That's exactly what I think God is saying with this virus. He said, "AMERICA, SLOW YOUR ROLE so that I can get you to your ultimate goal. Go hide in your room (house) for a short time until God's anger is complete." And so, many of us re-evaluated our lives, our time, and our talents. Some, God sent in a different direction; however, many others continued wearing too many hats, running too many places, drenching in self-indulgence, or being everything for everybody. Hence, returning back home empty and feeling unfulfilled - empty to ourselves and empty to those around us who actually need us to not be empty when we get home so that we can wholly and fully pour into them. But you know us, we can't stop, won't stop, and certainly don't want anyone telling us what's tops – top priority that is. We have minds that are so fixed on us and what we want in our flesh that so often we miss out on the ULTIM8 GOAL that God has destined for them who seek Him and obey His commands and directions. We are too impatient to do what the Lord says do for being prompted by the world to follow this and that and being challenged to do as others. In actuality, we do it and do it well, while falling short of the challenges received from The Challenger Himself, Jesus. Hence, we forever seek the desires of our hearts in all the wrong places, ultimately falling shy of reaching the goal that Christ has willed for us.

In reaching goals, we must ask ourselves, who am I aiming to impress, God or others? If you answered, 'others,' my question is, IS THAT YOUR FINAL ANSWER? If so, it's the wrong answer. If you answered, 'God,' then my question to you is, do you truly seek to please

God above all else? We can fool ourselves and others, but we cannot fool God. He sees all, knows all, and hears all. He knows the true answer.

As stated in Psalm 27, we must declare, "I WAIT ON YOU GOD!" There are some goals that are in my belly awaiting their expectancy season of birthing and I just believe as I patiently wait, God will be a doula for me and support me in my waiting, eventually delivering to me the ultimate goal, my heart's desire. It may be a solo goal, may be twins, may be triplets, but whatever the case may be, I truly believe God at His word when He says He will open the windows of heaven and pour us out a blessing that we will not have room enough to receive, as we do what He says do.

I am reminded of the Christmas season, and how Anna patiently awaited the coming of the Messiah for many decades. I can't help but think of how we 'new age folk,' would have handled that type of wait, or if we would have stayed long enough to even see the coming Messiah. From past experiences of standing in long lines at amusement parks, I can sure speculate on how our waiting would likely have gone. We would be complaining about hunger and thirst, complaining about the air conditioner in the Summer and the heater in the winter, oh, and complaining about the family that just jumped the line. We would ultimately become quite restless, tired, and frustrated. Many would lose all hope and just get out of the line and say, "Forget this!"

I can even recall the many times we have taken our kids to the mall at Christmas time and the frustration we sense when we see Santa, but cannot quite have access to him, except that we are willing to wait in the extremely long and slow-moving line. I thank God that even in our waiting down here, we are reminded not to be afraid, reminded not to move too hasty, reminded to take it all in, and reminded to feast on His goodness towards us. We are reminded to REST IN HIS WORD, which was left to guide us so that we are not caught up in the busyness of life and the human instinct of complaining and griping in our waiting. I am so glad that God is not Santa. When we want access to Him, we have it, through prayer, supplication, and thanksgiving. We can make our requests known unto God without sitting in His lap, without waiting in a long line, and without fear of anyone jumping the line. God is near to all who seek Him, and He stands ready and available to us always, even in our time of waiting.

23

P8tiently Awaiting the Appointed Time

Several years ago, when I was working on my doctorate, I had to speak at a church out of town. We were rushing on two wheels, as most families consisting of two or more human beings. When we pulled up at the church, I was finishing up writing a paper on my computer. I had just enough time to complete the paper and throw my laptop in the back so that we could make our way into the sanctuary. Well, unfortunately, as we were rushing the kids to get out of the car, eight little pitter-patter feet all stepped on my laptop due to our hasty request for them to depart from the car. Later, when I went to open my computer, I was greeted by about five large ink circles, which, over time spread into five gigantic circles. I spent the rest of my time in my doctoral studies trying to position words and sentences just right so that I could see between, above, and beneath the blotches because I was determined not to purchase another laptop.

For those who know me well, you know that I do not believe in spending money again on something which has already been spent. I am a saver, not a spender, and I can thank my parents for instilling that in me.

I was taught at a young age not to be wasteful, but to be grateful; therefore, in my gratefulness, I was appreciative that my laptop still worked and I was sure to not give up on it, that was unless it gave out on me. Well, I held out for many years, until 2020 when I began a wellness entrepreneurship business which would indeed require that I not have to look around blotches; or else, I may potentially be ordering someone the wrong health product or messing up their order altogether.

So, Christmas 2020, my hubby bought me a laptop. He bought it rather early when it was on sale in August. You know how we do. However, I was adamant that I did not want to open it until the proper time, Christmas. The gift stayed in the box for four to five months; and although I didn't open it until Christmas, it was just nice knowing that the gift was there. It was mine to have, and eventually, I would not have to continue peeping around what had become five humongously (if that's not a word, it is now) huge ink blotches. During my waiting season, it was a struggle to continue using my messed-up laptop, as it was inconvenient and it was unpleasant to my eyes many days. I was determined not to rush the process but rather wait it out so that on Christmas day, my hubby could proudly present my Christmas gift at the appointed time. Sisters, I told that long story to give you this tidbit, CALL THOSE THINGS THAT ARE NOT AS THOUGH THEY ARE ALREADY, because an appointed time is coming.

Jeremiah 29:11 reminds us all that God knows what's best for us, that God will prosper us and not harm us, that God gives us a hopeful future and an expected end. When, one might inquire? It is in due season, in God's time, at the proper time. So, the answer is all of the above, for God can and will do exceedingly, abundantly above all that we can ask or think. God can do all things! We are reminded in 2 Peter 3:8-9 that a day with the Lord is like a thousand years, and He is not slow about keeping that which He promised. He is patient with us allowing us all more time. The wait may be longer than the approximately five months I had to wait, it may be inconvenient, tiring, and you may think it unnecessary, but don't rush the waiting season because trust me, it is necessary. God is preparing you for the gift you will soon behold; but in your waiting, keep working, keep toiling, and keep pressing. Ladies, keep thanking God for what you do have, and do not take for granted what He has already done. Know like I knew that the promise, the gift, the blessing is in its designated place, right around the corner, in its keeping place until the Gift Giver, Jesus, is ready for you to open it.

Unfortunately, many are simply not valuing the time allowed in our waiting season. How long will we continue wasting precious time? We spend so much time doing things that we think will make us successful in life. Matthew 10:39 tells us, when we try to hold on to this physical life, we will lose it. God expects us to die to ourselves daily, as Paul said he had to do. When we are baptized, we are taken down into the water, dying to our old selves and rising anew, as Christ Jesus was raised from the dead. It is not just a ritual or ceremony for pictures to be taken and for family and friends to attend; it is a serious depiction of what God expects of us, and that is to die to ourselves and allow Christ to live through us in every facet of life. Is it going to be hard? It absolutely will be in many cases. Will we fail at it sometimes? We absolutely will in some cases. Will we get back up, keep moving, and press on? Absolutely! When God gives us time, He gives it to us so that we may utilize it wisely even in our waiting. We are to make His time be about Him in the time that He has so graciously allotted us. We mess up when we make God's time be about us, instead of all about Him.

In our waiting for the appointed time, we must use our God given time and talent to be about our Father's business. We don't just sit there waiting for God to do everything. God gives us all faith and He expects a marriage to take place with the faith He gives. FAITH + WALKING = NOW FAITH. Additionally, He expects that with the time He grants and the faith He gives us, faith and time might become one and birth a fruitful family of possibilities.

Remember Noah building the boat? Even in patiently waiting, only eight people were saved by God, being allowed to enter the boat of safety. God has given us plenty of time. In 1 Peter 3:20, we are told just how patient God is with us, even waiting patiently for the disobedient people to turn to Him. Even in this pandemic that we have now been in for over two years; God still patiently awaits us to come back to Him. John 12 tells us, when the people went out to meet Jesus and greeted Him as King; they didn't go empty-handed, they went with palm tree branches of leaves, waving victory in their hands. My Sisters, until that appointed time, as my husband often preaches and I continue to repeat, 'We Have to See It Before We See It.' Until the appointed time, we must see ourselves with the victory in hand. We must see ourselves overcoming. We must see ourselves in the winning season. We must rise like Lazarus from a place that may appear to be dead. What we may see as dead-end dreams and dead goals, God sees as a field trip – a temporary visit, a temporary situation for only a short time.

At Christmas time, we open gifts; we don't just hold them and look at them, admiring only the wrapping paper. We want to get inside the gifts and put them to good use. All of my close friends, who are like sisters to me, know that I will put what some may think as a not-good gift, to good use. I am appreciative of any and every gift that has ever been given to me; for in my opinion, no gift is too big, too small, or unusable. It is the same with our gifts from God. Whatever gift God has given you, use it in your waiting. If God can trust you with what may appear to be little or useless to some, He will bless you with much more in the appointed time, especially when He sees that you are putting your God-given gift to good use. Just like with our Christmas gifts, we want to unwrap our Jesus gifts and use them wisely, all to the glory of God. We must GET UP AND WALK with them. Take the Lazarus clothes of defeat off, get your blessing, and sport your gift. Jesus saved it just for you, for this appointed time so that you may be a blessing to someone else.

24

In Our P8tience, There Is Hope and Strength

There is a sweet lady at our church by the name of Sister Lyles. Sister Lyles is one of those people who is sweet as chocolate. She is one who has been the absolute same since the first day we met her. She has done so many sweet things for us, written so many cherishable cards to us, and has poured so many encouraging and uplifting words into us that when you see her, she truly appears to drip with sweetness. It is as if you can see the chocolate and the sugar seeping from her good and sweet soul. One of the many things that I have always admired about Sister Lyles is that she has always had a green thumb. If you were to ever ride by her home, during most seasons, you are going to see many flowers in her yard that are all bloomed and appear to be full of life. Sister Lyles, too, has always looked so blissful, bloomed, so joyful, and always full of life, despite the loss of three of her four kids, despite the loss of her husband, despite all of what she has witnessed in her lifetime of various social and economic events and changes. Sister Lyles has always held on to God and embraced life with hope. I have never seen her wear disappointment on her face or appear in distress. Even after she had a car accident towards the end of 2021, when she called to notify my husband and me of the incident, I could still hear the joy in her voice - the joy of the Lord that reminded her that things could have been worse, but the mere fact that she survived the accident was enough to rejoice about.

Sister Lyles has taught me, in my 16 plus years of knowing her, that even in my weakest state God will be our strength and our joy. God will be a muscle for us, as He strengthens us in our time of need. Where my limbs give out, He gives strength. Where I lose sight, HE GIVES proVISION. Where I cease, He starts. Where He leads, I will follow and where He lodges, I reside.

So back to Sister Lyles and her green thumb, 'cause I got all off subject. Pardon me! I just get excited about this sister because she has been such a bright light to my husband and me in our ministry at our church, as have many. I have mentioned all of the latter to point out that by Sister Lyles having a green thumb, she knows all about root rot. I imagine she knows how the plant gets root rot and how to prevent it because by the looks of her flower garden, over the years, she gives root rot a run for its money, because she isn't having it. I brought up this point to tell you, my sisters, root rot is something that we will encounter when our roots are not rooted deeply in Christ. Bugs can cause root rot. Uh-oh, somebody said they have some bugs around them that have been inching away at their roots. You know the haters, the naggers, the ones who drain you of all your nutrients that you need in order to flourish and blossom. I hear the spirit saying, "Loose your roots by letting those bugs go." Root rotters will delay you from getting to your destination. They will stunt your growth and ability to blossom into the beautiful flower that

God has planned for you to be - not just for your enjoyment; but to bless others as well. They will halt your progress and productivity.

So, I say to you, "Check those bugs and lose them! Secure your roots in Christ!" We must ever stay mindful of the very nature and condition of our roots. In our waiting for our time to blossom, we, like David, must delight in God, declaring before God that I will bless You Lord at all times and Your praise will forever be in my mouth.

In 1 Samuel 18, we learn that David had great success in life, not because he created his success and followed suit with everything everyone else did, but because he stood out with God. The Lord was with him and because of that, God granted him success. It had nothing to do with his likes, his followers, nor his loves because fact of the matter is David was just a shepherd boy. David didn't have all of that and he didn't thrive off of all of that. David came to do what David came to do and what he was called to do according to God's purpose for his life. David hoped for the best and David obtained the best because he brought 'The Best' with him on the battlefield. David ensured his roots were rooted in God and he did not allow the Sauls, his brothers, nor the naysayers to rot his roots - to rot his grounding - because this brother, David, his roots were securely and tightly knitted and interwoven in Christ.

In Joshua and Judges, we learn of a courageous girl named Achsah, Caleb's daughter, who asked her daddy for more; and I imagine she had no doubt that of which she asked for would be granted. She hoped for more with a bold and confident inquiry presented to her father, asking for a spring of water. Standing in expectancy, Achsah didn't just get a spring of water, her daddy gave her two, an upper and lower spring. She received more than she asked for. What a testimony of faith to all of us, God's children, that when we inquire of our Daddy in faith, which is basically the substance of what we hope for, God will provide the things which we have not yet seen and have not yet received. Eyes have not seen nor have ears heard the good things which God has in store for them who love Him, believe in Him, and are called according to His purpose.

When we confidently and patiently wait on God to fulfill His promises, we have hope that it will come to pass. That's true faith at work. I stand and walk daily in expectancy of the promises of God, for I truly trust God at His word. With faith in action, I believe it will all come to pass.

Jesus took his precious time going to raise Lazarus from the dead because He wanted them to know and believe that Lazarus was dead-dead, like real dead, like dead as a doorknob kind of dead; so that when He showed up and said, "Lazarus, arise," they would believe it was He, and only He, in His miraculous, majestic, and wonder-working power that had raised him. He waited until Lazarus got good and stinky, then He showed up according to His timing. Might I suggest to you, my sister, that even when that situation you are in gets good and stinky, don't you give up.

Isaiah 40:31 returns to my memory - to those who hope in the Lord, God will give strength like an eagle. They will soar, run, walk, and will not become weary, if they do not faint. When stuff stinks, we tend to throw it out; but don't you dare throw out the stinky circumstances you have been dealt, for it is in that stinky stuff that God will reveal His fresh aroma rising from the stinky-ness of life. Hold on my sister, THERE IS HOPE; and it is my prayer that you can see the light at the end of the dark sewer-like tunnel you have been wading through – a place full of stinky stuff, to get to the bright light, Jesus. Continue to PRESS TOWARD THE LIGHT, for Jesus is that Light.

As I end this book, I am reminded of what hope and strength feel like, for they both go hand in hand. Hope is a joyful feeling you have about something you deeply desire that you have not yet obtained or grasped; however, in your hoping, you know that it is on the way. Strength is our ability to firmly stand on the Solid Foundation, our Rock, Jesus, who gives us hope in all things.

If you ever find yourself in a place of weakness, my sister, I wrote this book as a friendly reminder, which you can revisit whenever you are in a place of weariness. I pray that it always brings back to your remembrance that in our weakness, God is our strength. I penned this book during a very trying time in my life, and the lives of many close to my family and me. In fact, I wrote this book during a trying time for all in this pandemic. In my journaling of thoughts and what God spoke to me these past two years, I felt compelled to share it with others who may be experiencing the same feelings I have gone through in this pandemic. God reminded me during that time, and I remind you; as long as we have God abiding in us and we in Him, we have hope and we have strength.

Every now and then I get a sore throat. I take for granted what a good and well throat feels like until I don't have it anymore. In an illness, whether it be a sore throat or a never-ending, nagging cough, we realize how too often we have taken for granted our wellness until we do not feel well. It is in our hope and desire to feel better that we seek God for healing. Sometimes we just wake up, and the next morning, we realize that the pain we once felt is gone. Sometimes we get so busy doing what needs to be done that before we know it, we realize we don't feel bad anymore.

My sister, one morning, you too will wake up and have in hand that which you have been trusting God for in your hoping. One day you will be going hurriedly about your daily routine, when all of a sudden, you will receive a wink from Jesus signifying that the door you had been hoping would open, has now opened and God is miraculously beginning to pour out blessings, which you will need more room to receive. We are reminded in Ecclesiastes 11 that as we sow and invest, we will receive a return. Your gift will make room for you sis! THERE IS HOPE, and God will supply that which you hope for and renew your STRENGTH to run on.

THE CONCLUSION OF THE MATTER

As we end this book together, let me remind you, my sister, that God is setting you in high places. We are but a vapor, a shadow, one of which doesn't last but a moment, after which it swiftly disappears. No sooner than we got here, we will be gone from here; hence, live every day as if it is your last.

I cannot close this book out without going to Zechariah 3, where Joshua is standing before the angel of the Lord, while Satan is standing right beside him ready to do what Satan does best, accuse him. The Lord shuts Satan right on down though. God says, 'Pump your brakes Satan.' Right in front of the enemy, the Lord speaks and rebukes Satan, inquiring of him, "Is not Joshua one who was once a stick on fire, but being snatched up by me he is now one that walketh not as he use to walk?" The Lord says, "Joshua get out of those filthy clothes and walk in the obedience that I will show you." He tells Joshua, if you do this, you will govern_____, you will have charge of_____, and I will give you_____! You can fill in the blanks, my sister, when you walk in obedience. In fact, God will fill in the blanks for you when you take off the filthy clothes, put on fresh and renewed, clean clothes that God gives, and walk in God's purposeful ways. What I love about this passage as well is that God says you will be able to invite your neighbor to sit under your vine and fig tree; and they too will reap what you have sown.

Deuteronomy 30:14 tells us that the word of God is in our mouths and our hearts. So, might I challenge you not to let it just sit there. Do something with it. Use it, tell it, obey it, follow it, and make it your business to be about God's business; then you won't mind people knowing your business, because it ain't your business, it's God's business. When we make our business be about God's business, we are not protective over our business; and we do not mind our business spreading, because ultimately my business is saturated and soaked up by God's business.

WALK TOGETHER sisters - in truth, trust, and totality of the treaty we have made in Christ Jesus, our Lord. The benefits are massive when we walk in unity, draw strength from one another, and stay in the will of God. Our strength and help come only from God and when God is in you, you have all because GOD IS ALL!

IN YOU, MY SISTER, IS STRENGTH.

Daily Reminders:

God Will Provide

In Judges 15, I am reminded of Samson, who after winning the victory, asked God, "Will I now die of thirst?" God then opened a hole in the ground, satisfying a thirsty Samson. Hence, we know that even if God must do the same for us to quench our thirst, He will. Ask Isaac how God sent servants to straight-up dig a whole well for him in his thirstiness. Now, that is a great God. If He must feed us by way of a raven, as He provided bread for Elijah, He will do that also for you and me. My sister, no matter what it looks like, God will take care of you.

Peace God Gives to You

Nahum 1:15 reminds us that there is peace on the hill and the mountain. So, I say to you, whatever you may be experiencing in this thing called life, look to The Hill, for there you will find peace and help in your time of need. Not by our own might, nor our own power, but by the Holy Spirit, working in us.

Exercise Your Faith

Zechariah 4:7 tells us that the mighty mountain is nothing before the spirit of God, who has the power to flatten it to level ground, producing a shout of praise to God. Exercise your faith, stretch it, work it, build muscle in it; hence, you will prevent injury from this thing called life. God can do all things and when we believe this in our hearts and confess this with our mouths, it will come to pass. It is not about what I can do in and of myself, but it is about what God can do in and through me, by faith.

Seek God First

Instead of focusing on self-seeking motives and opportunities, focus on God-seeking motives and opportunities because that is truly where your help will come from. It is worth noting again, Matthew 6:33 assures us that when we seek God first and set out to do His righteousness, then all these things will be added to us. In other words, all of our needs will be met.

Strengthened by Jesus for Jesus

Be ye not a prostitute of this world, giving all of what you got, which God has given you, to this ole' mean and hateful world. You might feel home alone, but might I assure you there is One upstairs, who hears your humble cry and He will surely answer by and by. We must pray Psalm 16:11 daily, Lord teach me Your ways for when I am with You, You saturate me with joy. I gain strength in the presence of Jesus. It matters not our circumstances, as long as we are in His presence. We know that He will fill us up, even when on empty. When my fridge gets empty, I know that it is time to go to the grocery store. When my gas light in my car comes on, I understand it to be an indicator that I need gas; but might I suggest, do not wait, my sister, until you are on E to go fill up on Jesus. Stay filled up. Attend Sunday school, Bible study, worship service, and seek God daily in prayer and Bible meditation. Feast on the word of God daily and refuse to become empty because your strength lies in Christ Jesus, so go get it.

Trust God with You

In Malachi 3:6-7, the Lord says return to me, and I will return to you. Yes, we are flawed, but who's perfect, besides Jesus? Yes, we face many difficulties and challenges; but hey, that's all a part of this thing called life.

DON'T FALL FOR THE HURT, BUT BE YE ALERT.
DON'T BE PETTY FRIEND, BUT STAY READY.

God is with us, Immanuel (In Man He Dwells). God has promised you so much and He cannot and will not stop until it is complete. Believe in and trust God with you.

Living Above Our Circumstances

When we believe, we belong. What we don't believe in, we do not belong in, as we are considered out of place. Living in pity means we are living out of place because God has not designed us to live in despair. Why live low, when we can live high in Christ and see the salvation of the Lord from a good view, above our situation?

We Have the Victory

When we fight, we fight to win, knowing that the battle is already won. Imagine showing up as a football player to play the game, knowing that the game has already been won and secured. This is how we show up on the battlefield called life. We show up knowing that we are not in the fight alone, that God is with us, that we shall not fear, and that the victory is already won.

Vengeance Belongs to the Lord

Isaiah 58:9 reminds us not to make trouble for others. LADIES IN YOUR DISTRESS, DON'T OPPRESS! You continue to BE THE LIGHT you were designed by God to be. We will be wronged in this life, mistreated, and ostracized; however, do not dare try to pay anyone back for the wrong they have done to you, for the Lord tells us that vengeance is His and He will do the repaying, so we do not have to. In Judges 15, we see that when the spirit of God is in us, God can do a lot with a little. Samson simply took the jawbone of a donkey and slew 1,000 men. When God is with you, folk can't touch you; but God will most certainly touch them, and it won't be for their good.

Sisters Support Sisters

Jeremiah 45:5 tells us not to seek great things for ourselves, for God will provide. You, my sister, just continue to walk by faith, seek and trust in God, and allow God to do the rest. Might I also add, help another sister out and bring her along. Birds go and find food for their bird family and friends; and we, having dominion over them should do nothing less. Even the ants find food and return to their ant home to ensure their ant friends and family are cared for. God has placed you in a position to BE A BLESSING with your blessing. Work well with others and as you grow in God and in grace, HELP GROW OTHERS. Help others embrace the gift within them. Help them pull their gift out by being the personal trainer they need to help strengthen them. Let us not give up on each other. Let us act in the name of love, knowing and living out the scripture, God is love.

The Growth Process

I am reminded of the process that a butterfly goes through. We have the pleasure of seeing the beautiful end result of the butterfly in its array of colors, flying gracefully through the air. However, there is a process that has occurred prior to the beauty being revealed. The mother uses glue to stick the butterfly egg to a leaf of a tree/ plant. Might we ladies be the glue, the connector that introduces others to Christ, our Tree of Life.

In addition, the mother cannot just stick the glue on just any leaf, as it is equally important that she chooses the right plant to place the egg because the caterpillar inside the egg will feed off of the leaf. Be careful, my sisters, as to where you are laying your eggs and who you are allowing to raise your kids because whomever they hear most in their ear is typically who or what will feed and grow them. We are responsible for ensuring that we are not only being the connecting glue to introduce our family and others to Christ, but we must ensure we are surrounding them with Godly, positive influences, for there are nutrients in the leaf, the Tree of Life.

Lastly, the caterpillar eventually sheds its skin many times during the growth process; and must I tell you, we too will shed ours during our growing in Christ process. We will go through some rain, storms, difficulties, trials, and tribulations, but it is all working for our good and in our favor. As we shed skin, God renews us, strengthens us, and character is built in us. Our hope is increased, and we have willpower to persevere. So shed the skin of fear, shed the skin of disappointment, shed the skin of hurt and pain, and continue growing in Christ. For when you are seen in your growth process, others won't necessarily see the beautiful butterfly which is to come, but that's okay because we want them to see Jesus in you. May others see what lies within and under the skin, what shines through the inner and outer layers, Jesus.

Good Ground

As long as a seed is planted in good soil and nourished with the tender, loving care of nutrients and water, it will grow. Luke 8 speaks of seeds that fall on different types of ground. If we are to grow in Christ, my sister, let us ensure the soil is right, fertile, and that we are feeding it with the Bread of Life and watering it with the Living Water.

Share the Love

When you step into your destiny, which is the will and purpose of God for your life, do not be like Jonah and want the compassion, want the blessings, want the forgiveness but not want others to have it as well. Ladies, utilize your resources to be a blessing to the masses.

Prayer

Father God, we thank you for the time we have shared in the reading of this book. I thank you Lord for your grace, mercy, and love reflected toward us when you sent your Son, Jesus, to die on the cross for our sins. Thank you for all the many blessings you bestow upon us. Thank you for your blood that covers us. Thank you for prosperity, for growth, for our home, family, friends, church family, food, clothing, necessities, and even our wants. I ask that just as you bless us, we will in turn not hold these blessings all to ourselves, but that we will be givers, doers, and blessers, taking heed to your word to clothe the naked, to see about the imprisoned and to love even the unlovable. Help us Lord God to grow in your grace and in your prosperity, not as the world envisions wealth but as you provision it. All these blessings I ask for all of my sisters who have ventured and shared in this book reading. I pray that each have been made better in their reading and that all will willingly and joyfully walk forward in transformation with the Trinity. In Your Son Jesus' name, I do pray, Amen.

A Note from the Author's Desk:

When God gave me the vision for this book, He showed me women ministries across the city, state, and nation being blessed as a result. Now that you have completed this book that I have longed to get into your hands, I pray that as you have been blessed, you will bless others, and bless the ministry God has birthed in me by gifting a book to a family member or friend. Just as God paid the price for you and me, let us pay it forward my sister, and bless the masses. You may even choose to set up a Ladies Transformation Book Club. Whatever you decide to do, always remember the fact that IN HER IS STRENGTH: The Her is You! Yes! IN YOU IS STRENGTH & IN YOU IS GREATNESS, which leads to my next book, "IN HER IS GREATNESS," so stay tuned.

In the meantime, I trust that you will share and spread the Love of Christ daily, as it is not ours to keep, but it's His to give away. God bless and keep you IN HIS STRENGTH, is my prayer for you.

Stay in touch with the Author:
Web: Getfitinthespirit.com
Email: drfelisa@getfitinthespirit.com
Facebook: @Lisa Marshae or https://www.facebook.com/lisa.marshae/
Instagram: @Lisa.Marshae or https://www.instagram.com/lisa.marshae/

ABOUT THE AUTHOR

Dr. Felisa Swift Washington is the daughter of Alabama State Missionary Baptist Convention (ASMBC) President Emeritus, Rev. Dr. Vernon Swift and Mrs. Josephine Swift, Women's President of the Northwest District Convention of ASMBC. She is a native of Tuscaloosa, Alabama. Felisa is the wife of Alabama State Baptist Congress of Christian Education President, Rev. Dr. C. Michael Washington, Pastor of Mt. Hebron Baptist Church (Acipco), Birmingham, AL; and they are the proud parents of three sons and one daughter.

Felisa is a graduate of The University of Alabama at Birmingham (UAB) and The University of South Alabama (USA) where she received her Bachelor's and Master's of Science Degree in Nursing, and her Doctorate in Nursing Practice Degree in Public Health Nursing Executive Administration. Felisa is a former Agency Nurse and the First African American Director of Nursing to serve a local school system, directing and coordinating the health services of over 19,000 students. Felisa wears many hats, as a Speaker, Teacher, Ministry Leader, Owner of Swift-Washington Jewelry Designs, Licensed Realtor, alongside her husband, Adjunct Nursing Instructor, Mental Health First Aider, NBCUSA H.O.P.E. Health Initiative Digital Outreach Coordinator, Wellness Consultant/ Business Entrepreneur of Get Fit Nutrition, and now Author.

Felisa serves her community and church through various entities of ministry work, volunteer work, and community service. Her heart desires to influence and enrich whole health and wellness by way of spiritual, mental, and physical health promotion, which she has the pleasure of doing through her Get Fit in the Spirit Health & Wellness

Business. Felisa enjoys speaking and presenting, as a Lecturer in the Alabama State Missionary Baptist Women's Convention and throughout her local city, state, and surrounding areas. Felisa is known for creatively and uniquely sharing the awesome news of Jesus; utilizing real, practical, everyday life situations to uplift the saints of God and to let her light so shine in a way that leads others to Christ.

Felisa holds the honor of being the youngest recipient of both the 2009 Martin Luther King, Jr. Day - Benjamin Barnes Branch YMCA Lady of the Year Award, as well as the Jefferson County Ministers' Wives 2016 Leading Ladies of Distinction Award. Felisa has been proudly inducted into and is a member or an affiliate of several city, state, and national Honor Societies, Incorporations, and Associations.

Felisa is always seeking an opportunity to serve God, her husband/pastor, family, church, and community to an even greater extent.

www.ingramcontent.com/pod-product-compliance
Lightning Source LLC
Chambersburg PA
CBHW070157100426
42743CB00013B/2944